CW00969529

EYEWITNESS AT
AMRITSAR

First published by Kashi House CIC in 2019

Kashi House CIC
27 Old Gloucester Street, London, WC1N 3AX
www.kashihouse.com

A CIP catalogue record for this book is available from the British Library
ISBN: 978 1 911271 21 5

Book design and layout by Paul Smith (paulsmithdesign.com)
Printed by Liberdúplex, Barcelona

EYEWITNESS AT AMRITSAR

A Visual History of the 1919 Jallianwala Bagh Massacre

AMANDEEP SINGH MADRA & PARMJIT SINGH

KASHI HOUSE

LONDON

I could not sleep or eat or even speak to anyone after what I saw. I wanted to go apart, and be alone.… It was a massacre, a butchery.… I feel that if only I could take each single Englishman and show him out of my eyes what I have seen, he would feel the same as I.

CHARLES FREER ANDREWS

CONTENTS

FOREWORD

By Dr Kim A. Wagner

In 2019, a new museum dedicated to the Indian freedom struggle was inaugurated at the Red Fort in Delhi. Among the historical events celebrated in the exhibition, the Jallianwala Bagh massacre, in which hundreds of unarmed Indian civilians were killed in Amritsar on 13 April 1919, naturally assumed a place of honour. Curiously, the display consists of a large replica of the red sandstone pillar that can today be seen on the site of the massacre in Amritsar, which was inaugurated in 1961. A hundred years after, the massacre is represented by either the abstract symbolism of its memorial or, perhaps more commonly, by the fictionalised re-enactment of Richard Attenborough's celebrated *Gandhi*-movie from 1982. A real sense of the historical event is thus notably absent from the way the Jallianwala Bagh massacre is thought of today.

Whereas the viscerally bleak black and white photographs from 1947, for instance, have provided a visual language through which we can conceptualise Partition, what happened in April 1919 remains somewhat intangible. In this volume, we seek to rectify this and put both images and words to the history of the Amritsar Massacre, and the surrounding unrest in Punjab. The images consist of tourist-snapshots, newspaper photos and illustrations, and photographic evidence collected by both British and Indian investigators. The words include eyewitness-accounts from letters and personal diaries, official accounts and police-reports, as well as the inquiries conducted in the aftermath of the massacre. Together they form a sort of historical collage.

There were, in fact, many attempts at photographically documenting what had taken place during the unrest at Amritsar. The official photographs subsequently taken by the British authorities were aimed explicitly at recording the scenes of riots of 10 April and the extent of damage to buildings and other structures. There was thus an almost forensic quality to the images of the burnt-out interiors of the banks or the particular spots where Europeans had been killed. These images are almost entirely devoid of human life, showing only empty spaces in a seemingly empty city. The photographs taken by Indian nationalists, as they sought to gather evidence of British violence, on the other hand, usually included people. Images taken late in 1919, by the Indian photographer N. V. Virkar, thus show local men and boys arrayed along the southern wall of Jallianwala Bagh, each pointing to an encircled bullet-hole as a sort of proxy witnesses. The horrors of 13 April could only be captured through the symbolism of the bullet holes, and it were these that left such an indelible mark on many visitors to the site of the massacre – then and now.

If the massacre itself was not captured on camera, the humiliating and indiscriminate punishments subsequently inflicted on the residents of Amritsar, and elsewhere in Punjab, certainly were. The snapshots taken by Sergeant R. M. Howgego, of the 25th London Cyclists, while on duty in Amritsar, are among the best-known. Howgego helped enforce the so-called 'crawling order' in the street where a female missionary had been attacked. With little apparent compunction, Howgego photographed himself and his friends forcing Indian men to crawl on the ground at the point of the bayonet. For these troops, the experience of being deployed in Amritsar provided a welcome distraction from the tedium of barrack-life, and was not that different from visits to various tourist sites in India where they also took snapshots as souvenirs. The final, and in some ways the most troubling image, is a group-shot of the eight men of Howgego's picket sitting on the steps of the shop in the street where they were lodged between 19 and 24 April. Although they are all wearing shorts and thin shirts with rolled-up sleeves, it is obvious that it is unbearably hot. They have taken off their helmets, two of which can be seen on their laps, but are otherwise wearing full equipment with extra bandoliers and their bayoneted rifles in hand. What is most noticeable about the photograph, however, is how happy and relaxed they seem and one of them even has a big smile on his face.

The 'crawling order' was subsequently re-enacted for the camera on several occasions and this iconic moment ended up becoming a source of British embarrassment as much as the massacre itself. There were also a number of photographs taken surreptitiously at actual floggings during martial law, especially in Amritsar and in Kasur, and it was thus the public punishment and humiliation, real or re-enacted, that came to define the visual repertoire of British oppression in Punjab during April 1919. It is of little surprise that the events of 1919 were later put to such effective use in the anti-colonial propaganda produced by Indian nationalists, and eventually also the Axis-powers.

Historical narratives can only be imposed upon past events and are rarely discernible to people as they unfold. Free from the tyranny of hindsight, the contemporary images and eyewitness accounts provide fleeting and often very partial glimpses of the past. They nevertheless capture something compelling precisely because of their impressionistic character, which reflects the different perspectives of individual experiences. In this book, we have sought, as far as possible, to resolve the lament of C. F. Andrews: that he could not show his countrymen what he had seen at Amritsar and so make the rest of the world understand the enormity of these events.

INTRODUCTION

Dangling like a bauble from the Grand Trunk Road, Amritsar emerged as a pre-eminent trading city thanks to the countless camel caravans that traversed the two-millennia-old route connecting Kabul to Kolkata. Located between two of Punjab's five rivers, and second only in scale and prestige to the region's thousand-year-old imperial capital, Lahore, the city of Amritsar owes its beginnings to a small pool of water said to be possessed with the power to heal.

The origin story of what would become the Sikhs' most holy site is found in the sixteenth century, when Guru Ram Das, the fourth Sikh Guru, halted at the pool after hearing a tale extolling its divine virtues. His excavation of the site gave rise to an *amrit-sarovar* ('pool of the nectar of immortality') that would become a place of pilgrimage and sanctuary for traders, artisans and devotees. Over time, a small but vibrant settlement arose with the mystical tank of water as its beating heart.

In 1601, a shrine called the Harimandir Sahib, which would house the first ever copy of the Sikhs' sacred scripture, was built in the centre of the pool. As the site's fame grew, a burgeoning city emerged that came to be known as 'Amritsar'. It came under attack in the eighteenth century from Afghan invaders as retribution for the Sikhs' refusal to acknowledge their sovereignty in Punjab. Though the shrine and pool were laid to waste twice in quick succession, the Sikhs were not so easily demoralised. They took the fight to the Afghans, secured Amritsar, and commenced work on raising the Harimandir Sahib from the ground for a third time. Defences sprang up around the new structure, with standing armies in and around Amritsar garrisoned at various forts.

The kidney-shaped city itself was encased within high walls and twelve grand gates gave access to its various *katras* or quarters. Mainly patronised and built by competing Sikh chiefs, they were akin to mini-principalities, each with their own personality etched out by the intricate maze of narrow lanes, lofty mansions and local policing.

By the turn of the nineteenth century, the Afghan threat had receded and Punjab was firmly in Sikh hands. When the one-eyed ruler of Lahore, Maharaja Ranjit Singh, took control of Amritsar at the beginning of the nineteenth century, the shrine and city were poised at the threshold of a golden era of patronage.

Between 1803 and 1830, Ranjit Singh commissioned an elaborate beautifying project that saw the Harimandir Sahib adorned with gilt-copper panels. It had now become transformed in popular imagination as a Swaran Mandir or 'Golden Temple', the latter being the name that came into vogue among Europeans visiting Amritsar in the nineteenth century.

Simultaneously, the city developed into one of the premier commercial centres, being at the conflux of trade routes and cultures from central Asia and the Middle East. Beyond the city's gates lay the legendary Grand Trunk Road, running eastward through the Gangetic plain beyond Delhi into Bengal, and northward past Lahore on to Kabul as one branch of the Silk Route. As late as the turn of the twentieth century, a traveller to Amritsar noted its vast array of peoples and the articles they bartered or sold:

> Amongst [the Sikhs] there was a great sprinkling of Pathans, and rough, hardy, picturesque-looking men from the mountains, clad in coarse garments and furs. They were usually traders from the north – Kashimiris, Afghans, Bokhariots, Beluchis, Persians, Tibetans, Yarkandis – who bring down the raw materials of the shawls and carpets for which Amritzar is famous, and also fine specimens of their own national manufactures and embroideries.[1]

This variegated populace was systematically documented in 1919. Muslims dominated, making up some 45 per cent of Amritsar's 152,000 inhabitants. Not far behind were Hindus who, made up of a kaleidoscope of sects and orders, formed 40 per cent of the general public. Sikhs, a perennial but significant minority of some 13 per cent, far outnumbered Amritsar's 'native' Christian population of just 1,500 or 1 per cent. Undocumented in this colonial exercise was a headcount of British Christians who ruled in the name of the king of the United Kingdom and emperor of India. Probably numbering no more than the low hundreds, what they lacked in numbers, they more than made up for in civil authority and military firepower.

British administrators, police officers, missionaries and their

---

1 A. H. H. Murray, *The High-Road of Empire: Water-Colour and Pen-and-Ink Sketches in India* (London: John Murray, 1905), p 312.

families lived closeted lives in the civil station to the north of the walled city. They dressed, ate, schooled, lived and worshipped in the same manner as their counterparts back in Britain. Despite almost two centuries of living in the subcontinent, to Indians the British remained forever foreign or *vilayati*, an Urdu term that, ironically, the Brits themselves ended up using to describe the motherland, Blighty. Protected in part by a sense of superiority, in part by the bifurcating railway tracks – which were in operation a year before the first trains began to run on the London Underground in 1863 – the parallel existences of Amritsar's colonial and Indian populaces was inevitably a tale of two cities.

*

British sway over Punjab began in 1849 when the East India Company annexed the territories of the Sikh Empire following two bitterly-fought wars. Within just eight years of conquering the last of the subcontinent's great independent powers, the British faced their most existential threat in over a century of empire-building. Their Indian troops or *sepoy*s were in outward and murderous mutiny, ostensibly on the grounds of being forced to break religious taboos, but more likely in an attempt to reignite the ruling pretensions of the last of the 'Great Mughals' in Delhi, Bahadur Shah Zafar.

Over four months of rebellion, the perverse ratio of the ruled to the rulers came into sharp and bloody focus as thousands of trained and well-armed sepoys besieged British enclaves, killing thousands of men, women and children. The failure of the uprising was in part due to the resistance (or loyalty as the British saw it) to the designs of the Mughal emperor from 'the Punjab'.

This fidelity was rewarded with a significant increase in the recruitment of Punjabis into Britain's coveted Indian armies – over a dozen new regiments from the region were raised during the desperate months of revolt. This preferential treatment was, however, double-edged as would become clear a generation later when the Indian Army was plunged into the European and Middle Eastern theatres of the First World War. Punjabis then made up some 40% of the men-at-arms in India's 1.5 million-strong military. Sikhs alone, though only 1% of British India, furnished 22% of the Indian Army at the commencement of hostilities. While Punjab's pre-eminent position as the Raj's most successful military recruiting ground brought its governing class great honour, its people held out hope for much more than just the economic benefits obtained from military service in the war to end all wars.

*

As Britain was experiencing a collective wave of relief from an end to the depravations and sacrifices inflicted by the Great War, the India of 1919 was eager for change. From the very outset of the conflict, support for the national war effort was evidenced in every tier of its society. Men, money and munitions had been supplied in the belief that somewhere within this arrangement lay some quid pro quo.

Expectations in Punjab were laced with bitter irony – the country's richest source of recruits had also borne the greatest number of widows. Furthermore, grain prices had rocketed, industries had collapsed, fuel prices had escalated and new taxes had been imposed. As if the economic storms were not demanding enough, the actual weather was no less relenting. Standing water from a heavy monsoon season in 1917 brought malaria and a deadly plague in quick succession. In a perverse reversal the following year, the monsoon failed to irrigate crops. The poor harvest was further depleted by the increasing demands of the Indian Army in Mesopotamia. Just when Punjabis could barely sustain another tragedy, the global influenza pandemic of 1918 swept across northern India. Suspected to have arrived on a troop ship carrying Indian soldiers home from Europe, the resultant death toll was approximately 17 million or an estimated 250 times more than the total number of Indian combatants killed during the war. A British Army officer breezily summarised this unforgiving period: 'The [flu] epidemic came after a heavy drought, when the village folk were half starved owing to shortage of food. High prices were universal.'[2]

For the Sahibs who ruled India, the situation was entirely different. The end of the war ushered in new risks to their iron grip on the country. Four years of warfare had proved a major distraction, disrupting the very careful social engineering that enabled some 200,000 Britons to rule a country of 200 million.

---

2 R. E. Parry, *The Sikhs of the Punjab* (London: Drane's, 1921), p 36.

*

By 1918, Muslims in India were being enthralled by the Khilafat movement, a last roll of the dice for the Ottoman Empire. While Punjabi Hindus were mobilised toward notions of *swaraj* or self-government by the Arya Samaj, a populist Hindu movement grounded in revivalism and communal identity, some Sikhs agitated to topple the Raj by means of an armed revolution. A conspicuously loyal majority in the Indian Army during the war, they had also provided some of the most daring and vicious opposition to it through the short lived Ghadar ('Revolt') movement. The Ghadarites – who, though predominantly Sikh, came from different religious backgrounds – adopted a strategy to entice Indian soldiers into armed revolt against the British, taking particular advantage of the vulnerabilities created by the Great War. This threat had been thoroughly defeated by 1915 yet the fear of anti-colonial conspiracies continued to haunt the British administration.

The prospect of dismantling wartime emergency legislation, at a time when hundreds of thousands of battle-hardened colonial soldiers were returning to India and wartime political prisoners were being released, was unconscionable to the British.

The sense of a threat from a politically-awakened population was all too real. As war-time emergency legislation was about to come to an end, the government appointed Sir Sidney Arthur Rowlatt, a British judge, to head an eponymous committee tasked with looking into political terrorism in India, especially in the Punjab and Bengal, and its links to Germany and the Bolsheviks. What those governing the Punjab sought was the same controls and powers that had allowed them to both quash the serious threat posed by the Ghadarites during the war and the judicial powers to clearly demonstrate to the wider public that those engaging in 'political crimes' were swiftly and severely punished. The committee's recommendation for an extension of the wartime emergency measures was seized upon by the British authorities.

The sheer political dissonance between the Indian population and its British governors was mercilessly articulated by nationalist leaders. Mohandas Karamchand Gandhi, who was yet to fully assume the fatherly role of the 'Mahatma', wrote in excoriating but lawyerly terms:

I have been unable to find any justification for the extraordinary Bills. I have read the Rowlatt Committee's Report. I have gone through its narrative with admiration. Its reading has driven me to conclusions just the opposite of the Committee's.[3]

Simultaneously adding his condemnation of the Rowlatt Committee and those that chose to violently oppose it, Gandhi instead advocated the idea of *satyagraha* or opposition through a higher morality.

In Punjab, and very specifically in Amritsar, the mantle of non-violent opposition was picked up local political leaders. Most notable were two members of the Indian National Congress: Dr Satyapal, a Cambridge-educated Hindu medical doctor, and Dr Saifuddin Kitchlew, an erudite Muslim barrister. With seasoned political acumen, they grasped Gandhi's message and commenced a series of mass meetings usually held at Amritsar's favoured gathering point – the Jallianwala Bagh. Satyapal and Kitchlew also gave a voice to the aggrieved by instigating crippling *hartal*s. Though a form of passive resistance, these city-wide strikes nevertheless demonstrated the ability and reach of local politicians while simultaneously laying bare the utter helplessness of the British authorities.

As the rising stars of the Amritsar resistance, Satypal and Kitchlew hit their zenith when the government pushed through the Rowlatt Act in March 1919. Its passage was met with a surging new impetus to their organised protests. While Delhi witnessed violence and rioting, Amritsar was gripped with Satyapal and Kitchlew's lightning strikes and even the very real possibility of the 'Mahatma' visiting the city at their behest. The latter would not be countenanced by Punjab's governor, Sir Michael O'Dwyer.

Cut from the same cloth of a century of scornful British administrators in India, but then hardened by the war, which had seen him shine as the architect of the most significant mass recruitment exercise across the entire Empire, Sir Michael was in no mood to entertain the notion of the lawyer-turned-holy man moving freely in *his* Punjab. To his mind, Gandhi's fanciful ideas of satyagraha were incompatible with the Punjabi predilection for martial behaviour: '[T]he people of the Punjab were not of a class to whom Mr. Gandhi's spiritual ideals would appeal and that they would translate Passive

---

3 H. N. Mittra (ed), *Punjab Unrest: Before & After* (Calcutta: Annual Register, 1921), p 33.

Resistance into an Active Resistance movement.'[4] He feared rebellion and revolution.

*

On 10 April, a hastily arranged meeting of Kitchlew and Satyapal at the residence of the local Assistant Commissioner deep within the British enclave of the civil lines was no call for compromise – it was instead a trap.

Just twelve hours earlier, O'Dwyer had ordered the two troublemakers to be deported from Amritsar. As they were hurriedly driven out of the city under armed guard, news of the arrests shot across the railway lines into the old city. The popular response, unsurprisingly, was a city-wide shutdown and the call for a public meeting at Jallianwala Bagh. Ironically, deprived of the moderating voices of the two leaders, the protesters lacked a coordinated response.

One sizeable group took to the streets with the intent to petition the authorities. With tensions rising, the thought of a mob crossing the railway bridges into the hallowed European civil station saw the police lay down an armed picket at the Hall Bridge. Their progress blocked, the angry protestors faced off against the police, who though armed were outnumbered and mounted on skittish horses. The first shots were fired just as the picket, which came under attack with bricks and stones, was in the act of fleeing in response to a crowd surge. Within minutes, two men lay dead as the mob penetrated the civil lines. News spread across the city accompanied by outlandish rumours that the British had poisoned the water-source and were preparing to attack. By the time Satyapal and Kitchlew had reached their mountainous exile in Dharamsala, the military had gunned down over a dozen, most shot at point-blank range.

The city's colonial icons became free game as angry protesting developed into freewheeling rioting and looting. Having killed a British guard and a soldier near the railway station, the crowd gravitated towards Amritsar's broad European boulevard, Hall Bazar. Bookended by the gothic-style Hall Gate at one end and the Town Hall and main post office at the other, and laden with British banks and businesses, it bore the brunt of the retaliatory violence.

---

4   V. N. Datta (ed), *New Light on the Punjab Disturbances in 1919: Volumes VI and VII of Disorders Inquiry Committee Evidence*, 2 vols (Simla: Indian Institute for Advanced Studies, 1975), vol 1, p 164.

Moving down the bazar, the mob stopped only to burn, beat, loot and humiliate anything vaguely belonging to the sahibs. Banks, churches, post offices and even the clock on Hall Gate were attacked. Bizarrely, the mob left what was arguably the most potent symbol of British rule virtually unscathed: a matronly statue of Queen Victoria.

Deep within the old narrow lanes of the city, a forty-five-year-old missionary schoolteacher, Marcella Sherwood, was pulled down off her bike by an infuriated crowd to shouts of 'maro Angrez' ('kill the English'). Severely beaten and humiliated, the attackers left her for dead. A local resident, Gian Singh, risked reprisals to tend to her, in part owing to the fact that both he and his daughters had been educated at missionary schools. This near fatal assault on an innocent woman combined with the murderous nature of the riots that saw three British civilians killed, cemented in the minds of the British authorities that they were potentially facing a near replaying of the horrors of sixty years earlier.

As the day drew to a close, the rioters returned to their neighbourhoods within the city walls, their fury satiated. British civilians, on the other hand, retreated into the imposing Gobindgarh Fort just a few hundred metres to the north-west of the old city. As the burned-out buildings smouldered, each side mourned their losses. Some twenty Indian men lay dead while dozens more were injured. Military reinforcements had begun to pour in and aircraft could be heard flying overhead as the authorities ramped up preparations to smother any uprising with superior firepower.

Tensions remained high the next morning as the funerary rites of the fallen gave cause for the mobilisation of an excited crowd once more. With the virtual collapse of civil authority, the military, headed by the newly arrived Reginald Dyer, stepped in. Born in India, this quintessential colonial soldier had served all over the Empire. He had been commissioned in the British Army in 1885 when in his early twenties. Stints in Belfast and Burma were followed by a transfer into the Indian Army in 1887. He rose to the rank of colonel of the 25th Punjabis, and was a temporary brigadier-general during the latter part of the Great War, during which he saw action in Persia and Baluchistan. Although a chain-smoker and racked by ill health, Dyer looked every part the stiff, efficient commanding officer who expected his orders to be followed to the letter.

Dyer arrived in Amritsar late on the 11th. An uneasy peace prevailed; the military was preparing to drop bombs on any of the funeral crowds that disobeyed strict orders, but both sides kept their distance for fear of reigniting the mayhem of the previous twenty-four hours. On the morning of the 12th, a forthright and ruthless Dyer led his troops deep into the city to assert his authority. Untroubled by civil legal constraints, his military column surveyed the damage, dispersed crowds and made arrests. If Dyer was buoyed by his successes in Amritsar, he would no doubt have been depressed by the reports from across Punjab of fresh riots and attacks linked to the Rowlatt Act, Amritsar rioting and the continuation of the satyagraha declaration. He believed rebellion was closing in and his brand of callous control could avert it in Amritsar.

*

What played out on 10 April 1919 would be eclipsed by the atrocity that took place three days later during a meeting at Jallianwala Bagh.

This irregular quadrangle of land, untidily hemmed in on four sides by houses and uneven walls, was situated just over a hundred metres to the east of the Golden Temple complex in Katra Jallianwala. This quarter of the city once belonged to a noble Sikh family that traced its ancestral roots to a village named Jalla. In the days of the Sikh Empire, their *bagh* or garden was a vital green space in an otherwise congested city – possibly even well-tended in the classical Mughal style, replete with orchards and water fountains. In 1919, however, it was a barren and undulating plot co-owned by over thirty individuals that served as occasional waste dump and scrappy grazing ground. Featureless except for a small shrine (*samadh*), a deep well and a covered-up branch of the Hansli canal that flowed from east to west to provide fresh water to the tank surrounding the Golden Temple, on 13 April 1919, Jallianwala Bagh was all set to be the stage for a momentous political gathering.

Local activists had been encouraging people to attend the meeting the day before. City dwellers were joined by farmers who had little else to do after the annual cattle fair had been suspended by the authorities. Their numbers were swollen by Sikh pilgrims who had travelled into Amritsar from around Punjab to celebrate Baisakhi at the Golden Temple (to commemorate a revolutionary turning point in Sikh history three centuries earlier) and to attend various fairs to mark the start of a new agricultural year.

Some of those who attended the meeting at Jallianwala Bagh that day did so to be politically sated, while others went just for the *tamasha* or spectacle. By the afternoon of the 13th, some 15–20,000 people, primarily men but also many children, had assembled to hear speeches as well as readings of letters from the exiled leaders in the light of the fatal shootings three days earlier.

Word of this gathering was relayed to Dyer, who was then stationed at Ram Bagh, a large garden complex to the north of the walled city that had originally served as Maharaja Ranjit Singh's official residence on his visits to Amritsar. The humiliation inflicted by this overt display of defiance deeply frustrated an already confrontational Dyer – the previous day he had dictated a strict proclamation banning public meetings in Amritsar, then personally marched a column through the city to make the declaration at various points to a bewildered populace. Now Dyer quickly ordered a military column to engage the 'enemy'. Entering the old city, he posted armed reinforcements at strategic points before heading towards Jallianwala Bagh to quash what he believed to be an insurrection in the making.

*

The detachment that wound its way through Amritsar's ever narrowing streets to the epicentre at the Jallianwala Bagh were made up of fifty riflemen of the 9th Gurkhas, 54th Sikhs and 59th Scinde Rifles. All were armed with Lee-Enfield rifles – a bolt-action, magazine-fed, repeating rifle that served as the main firearm used by the military. These riflemen were augmented by forty Gurkhas armed only with their deadly curved kukri knives and two armoured cars mounted with machine guns. Dyer was prepared for anything: from city-wide guerrilla attacks and deadly industrial-scale crowd control to close quarter, hand-to-hand combat.

It was approaching dusk when Dyer reached his destination. The meeting had been running for three hours and those on the very fringes of the immense throng would have been as oblivious to the political speeches as they were to the arrival of Dyer and his troops, or the proclamation read earlier in the day to insignificant audiences scattered around the outskirts of the city.

At what precise point Dyer had made the decision to open fire into the gathering is not clear. It may have been as he suddenly found himself and his fifty riflemen just a few metres from a sea of humanity caught up in heated political rhetoric. It might have been when news of this gathering first reached his ears at Ram Bagh. It could even have incubated itself weeks earlier when he narrowly escaped anti-Rowlatt riots in Delhi. Whenever it happened, it was certainly informed by years of colonial warfare and imperial policing, the likes of which taught men like Dyer to exert firm, overt and uncompromising control.

Mercifully, the narrowness of the entrance chosen by Dyer – an alleyway between two high-walled houses – prevented the armoured cars from joining the firing party. By all accounts, the well-drilled men took no longer than thirty seconds to assemble on a strip of raised ground stretching out from the entrance along the Jallianwala Bagh's northern perimeter. The chilling order to open fire was given without warning.

Panic quickly took hold as bullets immediately began to rip through flesh and bone, often hitting multiple bodies owing to their close proximity to the firing line. With scant cover afforded by the desolate terrain, some people threw themselves to the ground while others bolted towards the few, quite narrow, exits – one of which was locked. As the catastrophe unfolded, Dyer directed fire at those that surged towards the rear of the shrine for shelter. Volleys were also aimed at anyone attempting to clamber over the walls or up trees. Some managed to escape by throwing themselves into the drains that connected to the covered Hansli channel. Others found grim solace under piles of corpses.

Dyer's determination to send a two-fold message to the whole of India – namely the folly of rebellion and the acknowledgement of where true power lay – would finally conclude after some 1,650 rounds of ammunition (or thirty-three rounds per rifleman) had been fired for ten long murderous minutes. With that, Dyer's detachment lowered their weapons. Within an hour of having left their barracks, they returned.

*

The grim and heart-breaking effort to find missing loved ones, identify the dead and give aid to the wounded was severely hampered by the now very real threat that British troops would return to enforce the evening curfew. With vultures circling for fresh carrion, most of the dead lay unclaimed that night. Many of the injured simply bled to death where they had fallen. Others had collapsed in the streets as they desperately attempted to make it home. As many of Amritsar's residents slept unaware of the scale of the massacre, the British authorities made preparations for reprisal.

The next morning, while the city mourned its dead in a bewildered state of shock, Dyer wrote the first of several reports on his actions at Jallianwala Bagh. Given the unprecedented scale of the massacre in some two centuries of European empire-building in the subcontinent, he had single-handedly navigated the Raj into uncharted and tumultuous waters. Dyer's self-justification was clear and unambiguous: he had saved the empire from certain rebellion and murderous revenge that could lead to a bloody end to the British in India. He needed the approval of the civil governor – the equally imperious Sir Michael O'Dwyer. While palls of black smoke were still rising above the cremation grounds of Amritsar, O'Dwyer messaged Dyer from Lahore: 'Your action correct and Lieutenant-Governor approves.'

*

O'Dwyer's tacit support of the massacre buoyed the general, serving to validate his assertion that his appalling act was legal and necessary. Any fears that Dyer harboured that others may not be so supportive were misplaced. It would be several weeks before an opposition, or indeed knowledge of the event, started to emerge. The protracted delay between the bloodbath of the 13th and any official response was due to a number of reasons: the imposition of martial law, the commencement of the third Anglo-Afghan War just days after the massacre, and obfuscation from Dyer and others about what actually took place.

The traumatised and terrified citizenry were now subjected to a period of humiliation as 'Dyerchy', as one British journalist called it, came into effect. Anyone even vaguely suspected of committing, aiding or abetting insurrection and revolution was vigorously punished. Those suspected to have been involved in the rioting of the

10th were swiftly, visibly and severely punished. Central to this were the perceived instigators, Satyapal and Kitchlew, who were sentenced to transportation for life (though later released after a royal amnesty in December 1919).

Some of the most public forms of punishment were reserved in connection with the attack on Miss Sherwood. This relatively minor incident in the context of the wider violence that had gripped the city in the preceding week prompted an especially cruel response from Dyer. A military picket was placed at each end of the narrow street where Indian men had had the audacity to beat a European woman senseless. All Indian males wishing to pass the spot where the crime took place, including local residents who had tended to the injured teacher, had to suffer the indignity of getting down on their bellies in an act of evident penury. Pictures of smiling British troops enforcing this 'crawling order' at the point of a bayonet became a lasting metaphor of the indiscriminate cruelty of British power over India.

Less well photographed was the medieval flogging post that was erected at the site. Despite their neither having been tried nor convicted, the alleged assailants were brought to the scene of the assault while awaiting a trial to be publicly flogged. Even O'Dwyer couldn't stomach these acts of terror when they came to his attention. He ordered them to stop, prompting Dyer to relocate them to a spot outside the old city, where he insisted notable residents of Amritsar be forced to witness the whippings.

When news eventually seeped out to the rest of the country, it was received with horror and grief by Indians. The British response, however, was disbelief and denial. Almost immediately on hearing of the massacre, the Nobel Laureate and Indian cultural icon, Rabindranath Tagore, publicly renounced his knighthood, citing the 'insults and sufferings [experienced] by our brothers in Punjab'. On the ground, the extent of the massacre was only gradually exposed by an investigative team of Indian National Congress leaders who arrived in Amritsar in the summer of 1919. The contingent included Motilal Nehru, his son Jawaharlal, and the Christian missionary and social reformer, Charles Freer Andrews. Terrified into silence, the people of Amritsar now had a voice to tell their story. What resulted were photographs showing locals pointing to the bullet-ridden walls of the Bagh and countless stories of loss, horror and near escapes. Instrumental too was the local charitable group called Sewa Samiti, which conducted an almost forensic door-to-door logging of the dead and wounded.

The clamour for a formal imperial response grew unabated as public speeches stirred popular emotions, and articles and letters critical of the Amritsar affair began to appear in the Indian and British press. Some six months after the massacre took place, the government eventually yielded to set up an inquiry into the affair through the Hunter Committee. The move was regarded with deep suspicion by the British in India, who viewed it as London's liberal interference in their affairs. India's political leaders, on the other hand, held the committee to be a mere foreshadowing of an official cover-up. Consequently, a parallel Indian National Congress-led committee was established, with neither group working with the other.

Dyer's evidence in front of the Hunter Committee betrayed his fears of a reprisal of an 1857-like rebellion. In his mind, he was driven by duty, and he had both God and the British in India on his side. His job was simply 'to strike terror into the whole of the Punjab'. The Indian committee did not hear from British witnesses, relying instead on the testimonies of over 800 Indian voices to augment those gathered during the Hunter Committee. Both reports tackled the difficult question of the number of fatalities, a statistic that would become a crude proxy for the extent of the horror. The Hunter Committee calculated a figure of 379 dead, two of whom were identified as women, namely Bibi Har Kaur and Masammat Bisso. Fifteen of the victims were aged fifteen or younger. The youngest killed that day was eight, the oldest eighty. Drawing mainly upon the house-to-house enquiries, the Indian report estimated the death toll as being at least 500 and possibly as high as 1,000 based on an eyewitness who saw the massacre from a nearby rooftop.

The only uniting factor in both reports was a single concluding recommendation – Dyer's position as an officer in the Indian Army was no longer tenable. The Hunter Committee, which had already split along ethnic lines, deemed the general's continued presence in India a liability. Dyer challenged this assertion, believing strongly (and rightly) that he enjoyed the support of the majority of the British residents in India.

When Dyer arrived back in Britain a year after the massacre, it was to a hero's welcome. A public fund was soon established by the *Morning Post* newspaper. 'The Man who saved India' (as the paper, not Kipling, hailed Dyer) also had his defenders in parliament, who rose up during a ferocious debate in the House of Commons as he watched on from the gallery. The deliberations echoed the chasm of opinion between condoning conservative imperialists and disgusted progressive liberals. Regardless, it was a Conservative Secretary of State for War, Winston Churchill, whose chilling summary of the massacre informed the Common's resolution to condemn the British officer:

> Let me marshal the facts. The crowd was unarmed, except with bludgeons. It was not attacking anybody or anything. It was holding a seditious meeting. When fire had been opened upon it to disperse it, it tried to run away. Pinned up in a narrow place considerably smaller than Trafalgar Square, with hardly any exits, and packed together so that one bullet would drive through three or four bodies, the people ran madly this way and the other. When the fire was directed upon the centre, they ran to the sides. The fire was then directed to the sides. Many threw themselves down on the ground, the fire was then directed down on the ground. This was continued for 8 to 10 minutes, and it stopped only when the ammunition had reached the point of exhaustion….
>
> If the road had not been so narrow, the machine guns and the armoured cars would have joined in. Finally, when the ammunition had reached the point that only enough remained to allow for the safe return of the troops, and after 379 persons, which is about the number gathered together in this Chamber to-day, had been killed, and when most certainly 1,200 or more had been wounded, the troops, at whom not even a stone had been thrown, swung round and marched away.… We have to make it absolutely clear, some way or another, that this is not the British way of doing business.[5]

Mauled in the Commons, Dyer fared better with the Lords. Despite their overwhelming support, however, it was not enough to prevent him from being forced to retire (though without punishment) in 1920. He withdrew from public life to a cottage bought through the

---

5 *Hansard*, House of Commons Proceedings, 8 July 1920, Supply-Committee, Punjab Disturbances, pp 1719–34.

public fund, which had reached a staggering £26,000 (the equivalent of over £1 million today). The remainder of his short-lived retirement was racked by ill health and after a series of strokes, Dyer died in 1927 aged sixty-three.

Sir Michael O'Dwyer's retirement proceeded in a rather more orderly fashion, his departure from India in 1919 having been planned before the Amritsar massacre. O'Dwyer was essentially shielded from the worst of the fallout from the Hunter Committee's report and the battering from the parliamentary debate. Nonetheless, he never missed an opportunity to state the case for British control in India or to defend his own position during the troubles of 1919. This was most notable in his 1924 libel victory over a characterisation of him in a book by Sir Chettur Sankaran Nair, a prominent Indian politician, high court judge and, until 1919, a member of the viceroy's executive council until he resigned in protest over British suppression in the Punjab. The trial soon became a platform for a public response to the perceived ill treatment of Dyer by the British and Indian governments. O'Dwyer remained an outspoken and conservative commentator on Britain's role in India well into his retirement. He could never have imagined that the events of April 1919 would have revisited him in London some twenty years later when his assassin, Udham Singh, walked calmly toward him at Caxton Hall in Westminster, London, to shoot him dead.

The story of the 1919 Jallianwala Bagh massacre has been told and retold by subsequent generations. In family circles, political speeches, books, articles, film, song and poetry, facts may have inadvertently been mingled with, and on occasion obscured by, myths. Now, a century on, it is entirely fitting that the bloodiest act of colonial violence in 20th-century British India should be recounted in the voices and images of the people who were the eyewitnesses at Amritsar.

ILLUSTRATIONS
& QUOTES

‘ **The Sardars and people of Amritsar have never hitherto failed in their duty to their Government or to their country whether in providing men to defend both or in providing money to enable the war to be carried on or to assist in other ways.** ’

FIRST WORLD WAR RECRUITMENT SPEECH DELIVERED BY
SIR MICHAEL O'DWYER, LIEUTENANT-GOVERNOR OF THE PUNJAB,
AT A MEETING HELD AT AMRITSAR ON 17 APRIL 1918.

PRELUDE

1 The walled city of Amritsar in the late 1860s. At its centre can be seen the Harimandir Sahib in the blue-coloured amrit-sarovar. The empty piece of land to its right is Jallianwala Bagh. Beyond the railway lines to the north of the city walls is the civil station (or civil lines), and to the north-east, Gobindgarh Fort.

Overleaf:

2 A late 19th-century view of the Harimandir Sahib looking across the 'pool of the nectar of immortality' by the American artist, Edwin Lord Weeks.

3 The ebb and flow of pilgrims to the Harimandir Sahib in the early 20th century is captured here by the renowned photographer, Herbert G. Ponting.

4 An Amritsar street scene in the early 1900s.

Travellers Bungalow

Police Office

Girls Orphanage

Dy. Commrk. Office

Library

CHURCH

Museum

POST OFFICE

Railway Hotel

Boys Orphanage

Police Lines

Umritsur 0
Jalindhur 42 M⁵

E. T. Office

RAILWAY STATION

Sandras. T.

SERAI

Umritsur 1 M.
Jalindhur 42 M⁵

City Ditch (being filled up)

New Tank

Chapel

Rambagh Gate

JAIL

Jail Garden

Hathee Gate

Ernaul Sir

Sher Singh B.

Jobn Singh's Huveelia

Muhasingh Gate

Main Gateway

Fort

City Office

Mission School

Mooterum Sur

Santokh Sur

Govt. School

Lohagurh Gate

Ghee Mundy Gate

Lohagurh B.

Ahmeeolla Fort

Ghee Mundy B.

Soldier's Cemetery

Koorianwalla T.

Judges Court

Meean Shadee B.

Kala Duss Gully

Pai ka Kutra

Gulab Sing Tank

City Clock Tower

SERAI

Lahore Road

Akal Boonga

DURBAR TEMPLE

Minaret

Khazanwalla Gate

Chitta B.

Branch School

Mission School

Soolianvind Gate

TO JALINDHUR

Juloowalla

Kunnuk Mundy

Lchoongee Butter

Dispensary

Bubber Sur

Police Station

Dharmsalas

Lachmun Sur

Ram Sur

Hukeemanwalla Gate

Chateevind Gate

Phugwanwala Gate

Gilwalee Gate

1

5 Wood carvers of Amritsar captured by
the camera of Maynard Owen Williams,
the National Geographic's first foreign
correspondent.

6 Crowds pass through a narrow
Amritsar street in the early 1900s.

LOYAL ★ INDIA

"Among the many incidents that have marked the unanimous uprising of the population of my Empire in defence of its unity and integrity, nothing has moved me more than the passionate devotion to my Throne expressed both by my Indian subjects and by the Feudatory Princes and the Ruling Chiefs of India, and their prodigal offers of their lives and their resources in the cause of the realm. Their one-voiced demand to be foremost in the conflict has touched my heart, and has inspired to the highest issues the love and devotion which, as I well know, have ever linked my Indian subjects and myself."

King George's Message to the Princes and People of India, September 10th, 1914.

The King-Emperor as Colonel-in-Chief of King George's Own Lancers (Indian Army).

The magnificent rally of the Princes and people of India and their enthusiastic insistence that they should have a share in the defence of the Empire against German aggression is perhaps the most glorious chapter in the history of Britain's great Crown Colony. It was a revelation to the enemy and caused a chill in Berlin. The grateful acceptance of India's offers did more to raise the people of India to the height of the Imperial ideal than a century of just administration.

1. Franz Schulenberg   2. Ram Chandra
3. Ram Singh (on the left)
4. Dr. Chandra Chakravarty and Dr. Ernest Sekunna
5. Dr. Chandra Chakravarty in his Persian Dress

7 King-Emperor George V appealing to India in September
1914 to support the British war effort on the Western Front.

8 Some of the Indian nationalists of the Ghadar Party who
faced trial for their involvement in the Hindu-German
Conspiracy in San Francisco in 1917–18.

9 To bolster wartime recruitment, the Punjab's lieutenant-governor, Sir Michael O'Dwyer, made public speeches to gatherings across the region. Tribal chiefs, landed elites and leading notables were handed government jobs and strict recruitment targets that were met in part by coercion and threats. As a result, by November 1918 about 60% of the 683,000 combat troops recruited in India were Punjabis.

10 The 15th Sikhs was one of the first regiments of the Indian Army to fight in Europe in the First World War. This photograph shows them on parade at Karachi in August 1914 before embarking for Marseilles.

11 Remnants of the original battalion of the 15th Sikhs who returned to India in 1916.

' A vague uneasiness is troubling everything, and underground unrest, a communal tension.… The Rowlatt Bill is in the air. It appears to be quite innocuous, but Indians have suddenly discovered the value of propaganda. They are spreading abroad that meetings of more than two or three people are forbidden by Government, and other things like that, equally untrue. Henry calls meetings, makes speeches, and pamphlets are issued from the printing press in our grounds … but there is general uneasiness, unrest.… '

ROSAMUND NAPIER, THE WIFE OF THE GOVERNOR OF SINDH, ON THE
POLITICAL SITUATION IN EARLY 1919.

ROWLATT UNREST

"As I read the Rowlatt Committee's report and came to the end of it, and I saw the legislation that was fore-shadowed, I felt that it was not warranted by the facts that were produced by the committee. As I read the legislation itself, I felt that it was so restrictive of human liberty, that no self-respecting person or no self-respecting nation could allow such legislation to appear on its regular statute book. When I saw the debates in the Legislative Council, I felt that the opposition against it was universal and when I found that agitation or that opposition flouted by the Government, I felt that for me, as a self-respecting individual, as a member of a vast Empire, there was no course left open but to resist that law to the utmost."

MOHANDAS KARAMCHAND GANDHI EXPLAINING HIS OBJECTIONS TO THE ROWLATT ACT.

13 Dr Satyapal

14 Dr Saifuddin Kitchlew

'Dr. Kitchlew, in his concluding Presidential remarks, said that it was a pleasure to witness such a large gathering at the National Protest Day. Some men who convey false information to officers that the citizens of Amritsar have nothing to do with politics should know that the present large gathering was consisting of persons of all grades of society.… It was evident that the people of Amritsar aspired for self-Government and Home Rule.… He further said that it was unnecessary to shed streams of blood in the sacred land, but they should prepare themselves to disobey all orders which might be against their conscience and the commandments of God. It would not matter if they would be sent to jail or interned. They should prepare themselves for the service of the country and always act on the policy of Passive Resistance, even if they were attacked.'

REPORT OF A SPEECH GIVEN BY DR SAIFUDDIN KITCHLEW AT JALLIANWALA BAGH ON 30 MARCH 1919, AS RECORDED BY AGENTS OF THE CRIMINAL INVESTIGATION DEPARTMENT (CID).

Overleaf:

15 A crowd in Amritsar.

'We cannot go on indefinitely with the policy of keeping out of the way, and congratulating ourselves that the mob has not forced us to interfere. Every time we do this the confidence of the mob increases: yet with our present force we have no alternative, I think that we shall have to stand up for our authority sooner or later by prohibiting some strike or procession which endangers the public peace. But for this a really strong force will have to be brought in and we shall have to be ready to try conclusions to the end to see who governs Amritsar.'

LETTER FROM MILES IRVING, DEPUTY COMMISSIONER OF AMRITSAR, DATED 8 APRIL 1919 TO THE PUNJAB GOVERNMENT, WARNING OF IMMINENT UNREST.

10–12 APRIL

16 Chaudhri Bugga Mal. After Satyapal and
   Kitchlew were deported on 10 April 1919, it
   was Mahasha Rattan Chand and Chaudhri
   Bugga Mal, known as Ratto and Bugga, who
   organised the protests.

17 Mahasha Rattan Chandd

On the morning of the 10th, at about 8am, I received a note from the Deputy Commissioner asking me to see him at his house at 10am. I did not at all attach much importance to the matter and went about my daily rounds as usual and reached the Deputy Commissioner's house at about 5 or 10 minutes to ten. There was nobody outside. A few minutes after, Dr. Kitchlew also turned up. We had hardly to wait for a few minutes in the tent pitched outside when we were called in. There were a number of other Europeans. Among them I recognised Mr. Rehill, Superintendent of Police, and Mr. Beckett, Assistant Commissioner, introduced himself to me. The Defence of India Orders were at once placed in our hands, and we were asked to leave Amritsar at once. A few formalities having been undergone, we were put in two motor cars separately. There was a military escort with guns in each car. The cars were driven at very high speed and we did not halt till we got to the Nurpur Dak Bungalow [50 miles away].

DR SATYAPAL'S ACCOUNT OF HIS AND DR KITCHLEW'S DEPORTATION FROM AMRITSAR.

The news of Dr Satyapal's and Dr Kitchlew's expulsion had spread through the city like wildfire. Every heart was tense with apprehension, fearing that something dreadful was about to happen. Yes, brother, there was a palpable feeling of heightened emotion everywhere. All businesses had come to a standstill and a deathly silence had enveloped the city, the kind that pervades cemeteries. However, the surface calm was not without the resonance of the passion raging beneath it. Following the news of the expulsion orders, people began to assemble in thousands, intending to march to the Deputy Commissioner Bahadur and petition him to rescind the orders seeking the banishment of their beloved leaders.

THE POET, SAADAT HASAN MANTO, DESCRIBING THE ATMOSPHERE IN AMRITSAR ON 10 APRIL 1919.

❝ I could not make myself heard but the crowd stretched as far as I could see and they were continually increasing. There were three men who were in the front of the crowd running about. I could not make out why. The crowd were all shouting and behaving in a most fanatical manner, making faces, waving their hands. The first thing that I did was to go with the four men of the picket to the crowd and try and make myself heard, but I found that was impossible so I shouted out to them to go back and relied on my gestures to show that they were not to come forward. ❞

ACCOUNT OF RONALD BECKETT, ASSISTANT COMMISSIONER OF AMRITSAR, WHO CONFRONTED THE PROTESTORS AT THE RAILWAY BRIDGE DIVIDING THE CIVIL LINES FROM THE OLD CITY.

18 The railway bridge from the civil lines side.

‘ The horses were getting very restless and the man in white [Beckett] was telling people to get back. But no one listened to him. As the crowd was getting closer, the horses were being pushed back and stood beyond the over-bridge, on the road towards the Railway Station. The crowd clapped hands, and then advanced and faced the horsemen again on the road to the station. When the crowd stood thus, on taking the turn to the station, one horseman fired two shots at once and struck two persons. All people ran back at once. I also ran. Immediately after the firing, all the horse-men rode very fast back towards the Court Road. ’

LALA GIAN CHAND, WHO WAS STANDING ON THE FOOTBRIDGE A FEW HUNDRED YARDS AWAY FROM THE PICKET, DESCRIBED THE ENSUING CHAOS.

19 The footbridge from the city side.

" I was sitting at my house upstairs doing *tupa* [embroidery] work. It was food time and I came downstairs and saw a bare-headed crowd of men.... They were shouting out that Kitchlew and Satyapal had been arrested and taken away. They were closing all the shops as they went along. I joined them and we came along to the Queen's Statue Chauk where people said we should go to the Deputy Commissioner and have them released. We came to Hall Gate and our strength was then quite 5,000 or 10,000. When we came to the road bridge over the Railway line we found a piquet of British soldiers. There was a Sahib in uniform on horseback with them. This mounted soldier waved his hands to us to retire. The mob did not heed and insisted on advancing. Then shots were fired at us and we got back and wended our way to Hall Bazaar where the mob was shouting that some of their brothers had been killed and that we would also kill. "

TESTIMONY OF ASDULLA, A KASHMIRI WEAVER, ON THE UNFOLDING EVENTS OF 10 APRIL.

20 Hall Gate leading into the old walled city.

21 Hall Bazar seen from the top of Hall Gate.

22 The statue of Queen Victoria, which was spared during the riots of 10 April.

ERECTED BY THE MUNICIPALITY
IN COMMEMORATION OF THE
JUBILEE OF HER MAJESTY
QUEEN VICTORIA,
EMPRESS OF INDIA, 1887

22

INTENTIONAL CONFLAGRATIONS IN INDIA
SOME OF THE HAVOC PLAYED BY THE RIOTERS IN THE PUNJAB

AMRITSAR: THE BURNED RAILWAY STATION

THE PICTURESQUE HALL GATE

GUTTED HEALTH OFFICE AT TOWN HALL

THESE pictures give some idea of the destruction caused by incendiarism during the recent riots in India. The causes of the unrest were manifold, but chief among them were the fear that promised reforms would not be carried out, misapprehension regarding the Rowlatt Act, perturbation in the Mohammedan world over the fate of Turkey, the influenza scourge, which carried off about six millions of the population last winter, and a failure of the rains and a consequent very serious rise in the price of food. Of all these factors the professional agitators made use to the fullest possible extent, their object being to cause hatred of the Government, and in this way to promote Indian Home Rule. The ignorant masses are very credulous, and all sorts of mischievous and fallacious statements found an easy lodgment in their brains. The fact is, the mobs were inflamed by disloyal "intellectuals," by whose seditious machinations implacable anti-British feelings were deliberately aroused through an unreal, and, as is proved, purely temporary, union of Hindus and Mohammedans. While the rioting was of a serious character, after all it was, for the most part, confined to the Punjab region, where over a tenth of the area and about a third of the population were involved.

SCENE OF THE MURDER OF MR. THOMSON
the Alliance Bank manager at Amritsar. His body was subsequently flung into the street from the open window.

As Mr. Montagu, the Secretary of State for India, said in the House of Commons the other day, this showed the unmistakable and undismayed loyalty of the great population of our Eastern Dependency as a whole. A great amount of property was destroyed by incendiarism, and there was much looting and wreckage generally. Unfortunately, also, there was serious loss of life. The rioters did not stop short at murder in their mad excesses, and when the assistance of the military was summoned there were at various places collisions between the troops and the mobs. Altogether the disturbances, according to the latest estimates, were responsible for the loss of nine European and something like 400 Indian lives. The institution of martial law, which became a necessity in the circumstances in the affected districts, was wonderfully efficacious in suppressing the rebellious tumult. At Amritsar and Gujranwala, at which the pictures were taken, the rioting was very severe. At the former town, in addition to much destruction of property, between twenty and thirty persons were killed; while at the latter, where the post office, the railway station, an industrial school and the courthouse were among the buildings burned, the damage is estimated at between £50,000 and £60,000.

GUJRANWALA: GUARD AT STATION RUINS

THE BURNING COURTHOUSE

AMRITSAR: BURNED OUT ZENANA HOSPITAL

'I heard reports of firing in the direction of the bridge and saw from my house that crowds were returning. They were very excited and some of them were calling out, "Come brethren! They have killed innocent and un-armed brethren of ours, let us take lathis and avenge them." Some were seen with wounded bodies on charpoys. Some were running on with lathis.

After this, I saw from the top of my house dense clouds of smoke in the direction of Hall Bazar. My servants came in running, with the news that there had been reckless firing at un-armed people near the bridge, and, as a consequence, many were killed and wounded, and the people were enraged and had set the National Bank and other buildings on fire.'

PANDIT SARUP NARAIN ROZDON, A LOCAL CLOTH MERCHANT, OBSERVED THE CROWDS FROM THE WINDOW OF HIS HOUSE INSIDE THE OLD CITY.

23 British newspaper coverage of the disturbances in Punjab as reported in *The Graphic* on 2 August 1919.

> The crowd that had been shouting quickly returned in increased numbers. The first building demolished was the Post Office in the Town Hall. The office was at the back of mine. They broke the windows, looted the place and set fire to it. They left the Post Office and came to my office and smashed the windows. I had a loaded revolver, but happily the police arrived on the scene.... The natives, meanwhile, went into the Town Hall, pulled down the portraits of the civic fathers, tore them up, trampled on them and fired them. They treated every office in a similar manner, except mine curiously enough; but they burnt my bicycle.

THE CITY'S MUNICIPAL ENGINEER, P. E. JARMAN, DESCRIBED HOW THE TOWN HALL WAS SET ON FIRE, AND ITS INTERIOR DESTROYED.

24 The burnt-out offices in the Town Hall.

25 The iconic Town Hall.

26 The National Bank after it was pillaged and set on fire.

27 The looted store rooms of the National Bank.

Overleaf:

28 Coverage of the riots in Amritsar in *The Graphic*, 22 May 1920.

LOOT TAKEN DURING THE RIOTING ON APRIL 10
which was subsequently recaptured by the police.

FRONT OF
after t

INTERIOR OF RUINED BANK, SHOWING IN THE LEFT-HAND PIC

The much-discussed Hunter report on the disturbances in the Punjab last ye
rioting which was the cause of the terrible tragedy at Amritsar. After grav
a small military force, on Brig.-General Dyer's orders, fired on a huge crowd

TIONAL BANK
April 10.

BACK VIEW OF THE NATIONAL BANK BUILDING
after its destruction by the rioters.

Exclusive to "The Graphic."

IE SAFE (right) AND ROOM WHERE MURDERS TOOK PLACE (left)

peculiar interest to these pictures, the first that have been published of the
nces, in which two European officials of the National Bank were murdered,
bout 500 and injuring many more. General Dyer has arrived in this country.

"I reached a narrow lane where I was finally assaulted. My hat was first knocked off. I think I jumped off my cycle and a man picked up my hat and gave it back to me. I left my cycle and began to run and took a short cut…. I was attacked by one or two men who were coming from the opposite direction and by a number from the rear. I cannot say how many men were my assailants. I feel there was not a crowd. I was hit with sticks on the head and fell down. I got up and ran and was knocked down by further blows on the head and again felled. I was struck with sticks even when I was on the ground. I saw an open door and tried to enter the house but it was shut in my face…. I then fell down from exhaustion. I made one more effort to get up and did get up although everything seemed to be getting dark and I thought I was getting blind."

MARCELLA SHERWOOD'S RECOLLECTIONS OF HER ASSAULT IN KUCHA KAURIANWALA.

29 Marcella Sherwood recuperating back in England.

30 The niche where Miss Sherwood tried to hide during the attack.

31 Kucha Kaurianwala, the street where Miss Sherwood was attacked.

33

32 The Alliance Bank where the manager,
   G.M. Thomson, was killed on 10 April
   by the rioters.

33 The inside of the Mission Church,
   which was fired during the riots.

 First a howling crowd at the level crossing and on the overhead footbridge. Then a shout from [Captain] Gerry Crampton "to look out" as a bamboo stave came hurtling through the window out of which he had been looking. I had been looking out of the window on the opposite side – Gerry had done a smart step sideways thus avoiding damage. The train drew into the platform and a very agitated major appeared, who turned out to be OC Amritsar [ie Officer Commanding Massey]. Somehow we learned that there had been a serious rioting in "the city" – that one English woman had been knocked off her bike, beaten up and killed – that there were other ladies in the city – that the mob had begun to loot – that fires had been started and OC Amritsar had only a handful of troops to support civil authority.

LIEUTENANT F. MCCALLUM RECALLED THE MOMENT HIS TRAIN, WHICH WAS CARRYING 260 MEN OF THE 9TH GURKHAS ON THEIR WAY TO PESHAWAR, DREW INTO AMRITSAR RAILWAY STATION.

34 A train being stopped and searched for 'agitators' en route to Amritsar.

‟When the train steamed into the station here, the whole place looked like a regular Military post, with soldiers and guns scattered all over. The military consisted of Europeans, Baluchees and Gurkhas. On the main down platform, I saw a long armoured train. Some persons on the station, whom I knew, wanted to tell me all about what had happened, but could not talk freely, through fear. No coolie or conveyance of any kind was to be had. Just as I came out of the platform, Sardar Bikram Singh met me, and advised me either to go back where I came from, or not to enter the city in any case. Being extremely nervous, as it appeared to me, he did not talk to me long. By the kindness of a Railway servant, after waiting for 20 minutes, with great difficulty, I got a coolie to carry my luggage as far as the Golden Temple. At the foot bridge there was a guard of some European soldiers, who would not let any one enter the city without searching all things thoroughly. Sticks of all kinds were taken away from everyone.... At every step outside the city, one could see nothing but only Military or police at short distances with rifles and bayonets.... While proceeding to the Golden temple I saw marks of violence. Telegraph wires were cut, some buildings were burnt. Although shops were closed, the city was quiet, but every person looked depressed and terrified.”

GIRDHARI LAL, A LOCAL FACTORY MANAGER WHO HAD BEEN AWAY ON BUSINESS, RETURNED TO AMRITSAR IN THE MORNING OF 11 APRIL TO FIND THE CITY IN A STATE OF EMERGENCY.

35 Guard of the 25th London Cyclists desptached to Amritsar as reinforcements after 10 April.

Overleaf:

36 British picket searching all arrivals at Amritsar railway station during the aftermath of the riots.

‘ Hans Raj, ex-Ticket Collector, Amritsar, made a speech in which he said that as they had no leader to guide them, therefore every one of them was a leader. He also read a telegram from Dr Kitchlew saying that he was alright. The speaker remarked that he could not positively say whether it was the mischief of the Government or Dr Kitchlew had sent the telegram. He announced as well that a meeting will be convened tomorrow in Bagh Jallianwala, where letters from Drs Kitchlew and Satya Pal will be read. He exhorted the audience and said that they were prepared to make more sacrifice and would resist the Government. He also proposed that volunteers should be raised whose duty would be to inform the public in general of the arrests made in the city, and said that those proposals would be discussed in tomorrow's meeting. The suspension of business should be carried on, unless Dr Satya Pal and Kitchlew were finally released and the audience agreed to it. ’

A REPORTER WORKING FOR THE POLICE DESCRIBED A MEETING HELD BY LOCAL ACTIVISTS IN THE EVENING OF 12 APRIL, AT WHICH THE JALLIANWALA BAGH MEETING WAS ANNOUNCED FOR THE FOLLOWING DAY.

37 Indian Christian girls being evacuated from
     the missionary school at Tarn Taran.

38 The Alexandra High School at Amritsar,
     which served as a rallying point for
     Europeans during the riots of 10 April.

' At the meeting on the 12th, Hans Raj announced
that a meeting would be held on the 13th at the
Jallianwala Bagh and that Lala Kanhyalal would preside
over that meeting. He also announced that this would
be proclaimed by beat of drum, so that the people who
were not present at that meeting might be informed
and he also requested those present at that meeting to
inform their friends about it. '

POLICE REPORT FROM 12 APRIL.

13 APRIL

‘ The inhabitants of Amritsar are hereby warned that if they will cause damage to any property or will commit any acts of violence in the environs of Amritsar, it will be taken for granted that such acts are due to the incitement in Amritsar City, and offenders will be punished according to Military Law.

All meetings and gatherings are hereby prohibited and will be dispersed at once under Military Law. ’

THE FIRST OF TWO PROCLAMATIONS ISSUED BY THE BRITISH AUTHORITIES ON
13 APRIL DURING A PROCESSION THROUGH PARTS OF AMRITSAR CITY.

‘ 1. It is hereby proclaimed to all whom it may concern that no person residing in the city is permitted or allowed to leave the city in his own private or hired conveyance or on foot, without a pass....

2. No person residing in the Amritsar City is permitted to leave his house after 8pm. Any persons found in the streets after 8pm are liable to be shot.

3. No procession of any kind is permitted to parade the streets in the city or any part of the city or outside of it at any time. Any such processions or any gathering of 4 men will be looked upon and treated as an unlawful assembly and dispersed by force of arms, if necessary. ’

THE SECOND OF TWO PROCLAMATIONS ISSUED ON 13 APRIL.

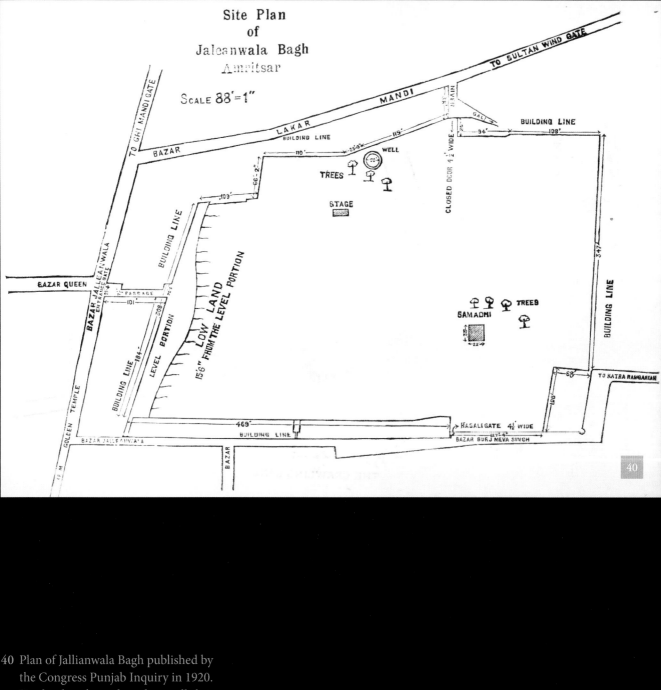

40 Plan of Jallianwala Bagh published by
the Congress Punjab Inquiry in 1920.
Key landmarks such as the small shrine,
well and trees are clearly marked, as is
the stage from where audiences were
addressed. The narrow passage leading to
an opening in the northern wall (left) is
the main point of entry into the Bagh.

❛ The word *bagh* [garden] is particularly misleading in the denomination; in fact it is a positive misnomer. The *Jalyanwalla* [Bagh] bears no resemblance to a garden. On the contrary, it is something like what we call a *kharhar* [wasteland], extending over 250 yds in length and over 200 in breadth. On the north side of the vast *maidan* [open space] there is a raised platform of earth, more accurately, a *tila* [high ground] which runs from one end of it to the other.… On three sides, walls of the adjacent houses surround the maidan like a fortress and the little space which is uncovered by house walls is enclosed by a *kaccha* [mud] fence over 5 ft in height.… There are no proper doors to the maidan, but there are five crevices or shabby lanes on different sides which for the purposes of ingress and egress to it, may be exalted to the dignity of doors!… The doors lead to small lanes that are anything but wide and moreover, full of sewer *nalies* [open drains]. In the middle of the kharhar stands a small dilapidated temple, and far on the east side, is situated underneath a couple of big banyan trees a well with an unusually big circumference. ❜

A DESCRIPTION OF JALLIANWALA BAGH BY THE INDIAN JOURNALIST,
KAPIL DEVA MALAVIYA.

‘ On the 13th of April 1919, I heard it announced by the beat of drum that Lala Kanhiyalal, Vakil [lawyer], would deliver a lecture in the Jallianwala Bagh that evening. As the Bazar was closed and I had nothing to do, I went to the garden at 3pm with my son, son-in-law and a few other boys, some of whom were children of 7 or 8 years only.

I did not see or hear of any announcement by beat of drum, or proclamation or notice that people were prohibited from attending public meetings, or that such a meeting would be broken up by force. That was the reason why I went with the boys and children of my family.

A little after my reaching the garden, I noticed an aeroplane hovering over there for some time and returning after a few rounds. ’

A LOCAL RESIDENT OF AMRITSAR, THE SIXTY-YEAR-OLD MULCHAND, WENT TO THE BAGH WITH THE YOUNGER BOYS OF HIS FAMILY EXPECTING TO HEAR A RESPECTED LOCAL LAWYER GIVE A LECTURE.

42

‘ I was watching the meeting at Jallianwala Bagh, on April 13th from the roof of a temple close by.… I saw a Sikh addressing a huge gathering of about 20,000. People were continuously pouring in from all the openings into the garden, I saw a number of children sitting on the shoulders of the men assembled. There was a very large number of Jats, who had come from distant villages to join the "Baisakhi fair" at Amritsar. ’

THE FIFTEEN-YEAR-OLD LALA PARMANAND, WHO LIVED NEARBY THE BAGH, DESCRIBED THE CROWDS THAT GATHERED THAT DAY.

‘ In the Bagh, there was a very large crowd, so big that people could not hear. There were many of those who could not hear, who were sitting on the grass and the children were playing about.… It was the Baisakhi Festival and the shops were closed and there was nothing to do, and when the lecture was announced, the people came there. Some people were sitting down playing cards. Some were coming, others were going. Many people had come from the country, as far as from Peshawar and Rawalpindi, because it was the Baisakhi fair. ’

LALA KARAM CHAND, A LOCAL BANK ACCOUNTANT, WENT WITH A FRIEND TO THE BAGH.

1. This grand meeting of the inhabitants of Amritsar looks with extreme indignation and disapproval on all those revolutionary actions which are the inevitable result of the inappropriate and inequitable attitude on the part of the Government, and entertains apprehension that this despotic conduct of the Government might prove deleterious to the British Government.

2. This grand meeting of the inhabitants of Amritsar strongly protests against the despotic attitude which the Government adopted when the subject-people within the domains of law invited the attention of the British subjects by means of the only effective and last expedient, i.e. "passive resistance" to improper legislation of the Government of India, i.e. the Rowlatt Act, which was passed in disregard of the united voice of the public.

3. This grand meeting gives expression to its heartfelt and sincere sympathy with the families of the philanthropic and patriotic personages, Dr. Saif ud Din Kitchlew and Dr. Satya Pal, on their deportation by the Government, which is being naturally and inevitably felt by the members of those families.

4. This meeting gives expression to its feeling of displeasure on, and strongly protests against, the deportation of the popular patriots, Dr. Saif ud Din Kitchlew and Dr. Satya Pal, and, while keeping in view the injurious effects of the despotic attitude of the Government, which is simply based on one-sided and unauthenticated reports, requests that all the persons deported and interned may be released without any further delay.

5. Copies of the resolutions to be sent to … the Secretary of State, the Viceroy, the Lieutenant-Governor of the Punjab, and the Deputy Commissioner of Amritsar, and a copy of resolution No. 4 be sent to the families of both the respective deported leaders.

THE RESOLUTIONS PREPARED BY THE ORGANISERS OF THE MEETING AT JALLIANWALA BAGH ON 13 APRIL 1919. THE THIRD ONE WAS BEING READ OUT WHEN DYER ARRIVED.

44

43, 44 Views of the Bagh towards the
southern-end wall, with the small
shrine in the middle.

‘ I knew that the final crisis had come, and that the assembly was primarily of the same mobs which had murdered and looted and burnt three days previously, and showed their truculence and contempt of the troops during the intervening days, that it was a deliberate challenge to the Government forces, and that if it were not dispersed effectively, with sufficient impression upon the designs and arrogance of the rebels and their followers we should be overwhelmed during the night or the next day by a combination of the city gangs and of the still more formidable multitude from the villages. ’

GENERAL R. E. H. DYER'S ASSESSMENT OF THE MEETING AT JALLIANWALA BAGH.

45 General Reginald Dyer at the time of the
Hunter Committee inquiry, November 1919.

Shortly after 4pm I matured my plans and leaving a reserve for emergencies I marched with the piquetting parties and a special party consisting of 25 rifles, 1/9th Gurkhas, 25 rifles, 54th Sikhs, F.F. [ie Frontier Force] and 59th Rifles, F.F. and two armoured cars. There were also 40 Gurkhas armed only with "kukris" with the special party. These were all the troops available after providing for the piquets, reserves, and duties. I proceeded through the city towards the Jallianwala Bagh at the usual pace, dropping my piquetting parties as I marched. The gathering in the Jallianwala Bagh must have received ample warning of my coming, and I personally had ample time to consider the nature of the painful duty I might be faced with. '

THE PLAN OF ACTION DEVISED BY DYER ON 13 APRIL 1919.

47

❝ The party was led to Jallianwalah Bagh by a guide, and arrived at a small alley just about broad enough for two men walking abreast. This necessitated leaving the two armoured cars behind.… The General Officer Commanding [Dyer], Colonel Morgan, Mr Rehill and myself got out of the motor and advanced up the alley, the troops following us. Coming to the end of the alley we saw an immense crowd of men packed in a square, listening to a man on a platform who was speaking and gesticulating with his hands. It was very hard to estimate the size of the crowd. The General asked me what I thought the numbers were, and I said about 5,000. ❞

CAPTAIN F. BRIGGS, DYER'S BRIGADE-MAJOR, DESCRIBED THE MOMENT THEY ENTERED JALLIANWALA BAGH.

48 The narrow passage leading into Jallianwala Bagh on the northern side.

With the foregoing considerations before me and the daily reports and sights of Amritsar itself, I had no doubt that I was dealing with no mere local disturbance but a rebellion, which, whatever its origin, was aiming at something wide reaching and vastly more serious even than local riots and looting. The isolation of centres and the holding up of the movement of military reserves by destroying communications were essential features of the conspiracy.

I was conscious of a great offensive movement gathering against me, and knew that to sit still and await its complete mobilization would be fatal. When, therefore, the express challenge by this movement in the shape of the assembly in the Jallianwallah Bagh came to me, I knew a military crisis had come, and that to view the assembly as a mere political gathering, requiring simply to be induced to go away because it was there in breach of an order, was wholly remote from the facts and the necessities of the case.

Amritsar was in fact the storm centre of a rebellion. The whole Punjaub had its eyes on Amritsar, and the assembly of the crowd that afternoon was for all practical purposes a declaration of war by leaders whose hope and belief was that I should fail to take up the challenge. **)**

DYER'S ACCOUNT OF THE SITUATION THAT HE FACED AT AMRITSAR.

49 The position along the northern wall from where Dyer's troops opened fire.

50

‘ When fire was opened the whole crowd seemed to sink to the ground, a whole flutter of white garments, with however a spreading out towards the main gateway, and some individuals could be seen climbing the high wall. There was little movement, except for the climbers. The gateway would soon be jammed. I saw no sign of a rush towards the troops. After a bit, I noticed that Captain Briggs was drawing up his face as if in pain, and was plucking at the general's elbow. Mr. Plomer, Deputy Superintendent of Police, told the General during a lull that he had taught the crowd a lesson they would never forget. The General took no notice, and ordered fire to be resumed, directing it particularly at the wall. ’

SERGEANT W. J. ANDERSON, DYER'S PERSONAL BODYGUARD, DESCRIBED WHAT HAPPENED AFTER THE ORDER TO FIRE WAS GIVEN.

‘We went running at once to the right, where there is a passage. I rushed towards the passage and heard the soldiers firing. There were many who rushed there before me and after me. The people were all running when the firing began. The soldiers came in and formed into a line at once, and there was no warning given at all. They began to fire at once. I was near the Hansli passage when the firing began. The end of the passage was blocked by a wall as high as my chest, and so people could not get out quickly, but only one by one. When I got into the passage, I saw that people were being shot down behind me. I tried to crouch down and saw that the trap door of the Hansli was broken. So, in the crush, I managed to get down into it, one leg at the time. I got into the water up to my thigh at the place where the lid over it was broken. Three other men slipped in.’

LALA KARAM CHAND AND A FRIEND RAN FOR COVER TOWARDS THE NORTH-EASTERN CORNER WHEN THE MAIN ENTRANCE WAS BLOCKED BY THE SOLDIERS.

❝ [I] pulled down my son. Many shots came whistling and men began to fall as they were running away. My son and I lay down at full length. Those who had war experience, shouted out, "Lie flat." When the firing ceased, men who were lying flat got up and began to run. I ran also. When the men began to run, the shots began again. I lay down flat with my son. Then for the second time the shots ceased. Men began to run again and I ran and got to the other side of the platform and fell flat there. There was quite a heap of bodies and I was protected from the bullets by them... The bodies were so thick about the passage, that I could not find my way out. I had my son with me and men were rushing over the dead bodies.... Nearly all my clothes were left behind.... The *pagri* (turban) and shoes of my son were also lost. As I was creeping near the dead bodies, I slipped and fell and lost hold of my son.

The people behind, now began trampling over me, and I had many blows and wounds on my chest. All my breath was taken out of me and I thought I was dying. When the rush was over, I revived and got out from amongst the dead bodies and ran into the lane. I had no dhotie, only a shirt and a coat I had. I could not speak. I was stunned and went into some house. I don't know whose it was. Just then I heard someone saying, "They are coming again; they are coming again." I rushed out and fled down another lane. On the road I was so thirsty that I could not run or stand any more. I took some water from an old woman at the well and asked for a *langotee* (loin cloth). Then I began crying "Has anyone seen my child," but no one had seen him. I ran home and found my son had not reached there. My relations went in all directions to find him. After half an hour the boy came back himself. 〉

THIRTY-THREE-YEAR-OLD PERFUME-MAKER, PRATAP SINGH, WAS SITTING NEAR THE
SPEAKERS' PLATFORM WITH HIS SON WHEN THE SHOOTING BEGAN.

❝ I fired and continued to fire until the crowd dispersed and I consider this is the least amount of firing which would produce the necessary moral and widespread effect it was my duty to produce, if I was to justify my action. If more troops had been at hand the casualties would be greater in proportion. *It was no longer a question of merely dispersing the crowd*; but one of producing a sufficient moral effect, from a military point of view, not only on those who were present but more specially throughout the Punjab. There could be no question of undue severity. ❞

THE LOGIC BEHIND DYER'S ACTIONS AS HE LATER EXPLAINED IT IN AN OFFICIAL REPORT.

❝ The firing continued incessantly for about 10 to 15 minutes at least, without any perceptible break. I saw hundreds or persons killed on the spot. In the Bagh there were about 12 to 15 thousand persons and they consisted of many villagers, who had come to Amritsar to see the Baisakhi fair. The worst part of the whole thing was that the firing was directed towards the gates through which the people running out. There were small outlets, four or five in all, and bullets actually rained over the people at all these gates. Shots were fired into the thick of the meeting. There was not a corner left of the garden facing the firing line, where people did not die in large numbers. Many got trampled under the feet of the rushing crowds and thus lost their lives. Blood was pouring in profusion. Even those who lay flat on the ground were shot, as I saw the Gurkhas kneel down and fire. As soon as the firing stopped, the troops and officers all cleared away. ❞

FROM THE VANTAGE-POINT OF A NEARBY ROOFTOP, GIRDHARI LAL WITNESSED THE MASSACRE TAKING PLACE JUST A FEW HUNDRED FEET AWAY.

Overleaf:

52 Panorama of Jallianwala Bagh showing
the eastern and southern walls.

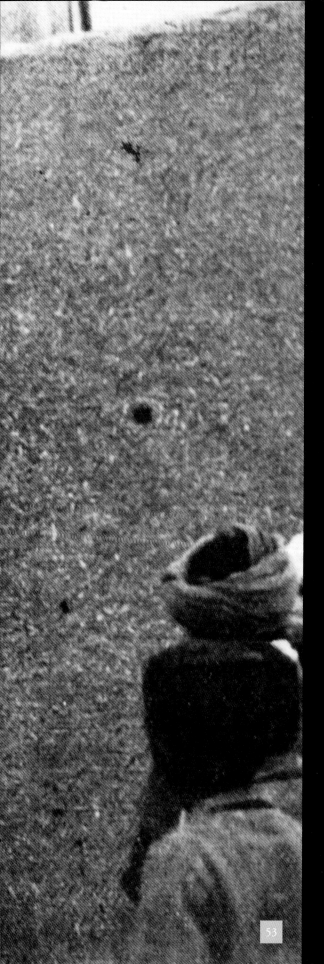

'After the soldiers had left, I looked round.... There must have been more than a thousand corpses there. The whole place was strewn with them. At some places, 7 or 8 corpses were piled, one over another. In addition to the dead, there must have been about a thousand wounded persons lying there. Close by where I was lying, I saw a young boy, aged about 12 years, lying dead with a child of about 3 years clasped in his arms, also dead.'

HAVING BEEN SHOT TWICE IN THE LEG, LALA GURANDITTA DRAGGED HIMSELF TO AN UPRIGHT POSITION AND SURVEYED THE CARNAGE.

53 Locals inspecting bullet-holes in the southern wall, behind the shrine, in late 1919. This and the next photograph were later published in *L'Illustration* in March 1920.

‘I saw people were hurrying up, and many had to leave their dead and wounded, because they were afraid of being fired upon again after [the curfew at] 8pm. Many amongst the wounded, who managed to run away from the garden, succumbed on their way to the injuries received, and lay dead in the streets.’

AS NIGHT WAS APPROACHING, GIRDHARI LAL WENT INTO THE BAGH TO HELP LOOK FOR A NEIGHBOUR'S SONS.

4 A speaker addressing a crowd from behind the lowest part of the southern wall in late 1919.

54

‘I was aware that the inhabitants had been warned they were not to hold meetings or followings, and that if they did so they would be fired on. To further enforce my wishes, a proclamation was proclaimed on morning of 13th by beat of drum in many of the main streets of the city, warning the inhabitants that unlawful acts would be punished by military force. On my way back from the city I was informed that the disaffected characters of the city had ordered a meeting in the Jallianwallah Bagh at 16.30 hours. I did not think this meeting would take place in the face of what I had done.

At 16.00 hours I received a report from the police that a gathering was beginning in the place mentioned above.

I immediately sent picquets to hold various gates of the city and marched with 25 rifles, 9th Gurkhas, and 25 rifles from detachments of 54th Sikhs F.F. and 59th Rifles F.F. making a total of 50 rifles, and also 40 Gurkhas armed with *kukris*. Two armoured cars also accompanied this party.

I entered the Jallianwallah Bagh by a very narrow lane which necessitated my leaving my armoured cars behind.

On entering I saw a dense crowd estimated at about 5,000; a man on a raised platform addressing the audience and making gesticulation with his hands…

…I realized that my force was small and to hesitate might induce attack. I immediately opened fire and dispersed the crowd.

I estimate between 200 and 300 of the crowd were killed. My party fired 1,650 rounds.

I returned to my Headquarters about 18.00 hours.

At 22.00 hours accompanied by a force, I visited all my picquets and marched through the city in order to make sure that my orders as to inhabitants not being out of their houses after 20.00 had been obeyed.

The city was absolutely quiet and not a soul to be seen.

I returned to Headquarters at midnight. The inhabitants have asked permission to bury the dead in accordance with my orders. This I am allowing.

Your most obedient Servant
R. E. Dyer
Brig.-General, Commanding 45th Brigade

DYER'S REPORT TO HIS SUPERIOR, MAJOR-GENERAL WILLIAM BEYNON, WRITTEN THE DAY AFTER THE MASSACRE.

‘ I was in my house near Jallianwala Bagh when I heard shots fired…. I got up at once as I was anxious because my husband had gone to the Bagh. I began to cry, and went to the place accompanied by two women to help me. There I saw heaps of dead bodies and I began to search for my husband. After passing through that heap, I found the dead body of my husband. The way towards it was full of blood and dead bodies. After a short time, both the sons of Lala Sundar Das came there; and I asked them to bring a *charpai* (cot) to carry the dead body of my husband home. The boys accordingly went home and I sent away the two women also. By this time, it was 8 o'clock and no one could stir out of his house, because of the curfew order. I stood waiting and crying…

…[I] seated myself by the side of my dead husband. Accidentally, I found a bamboo stick which I kept in my hand to keep off dogs. I saw three men writhing in agony, a buffalo struggling in great pain; and a boy, about 12 years old, in agony entreated me not to leave the place. I told him that I could not go anywhere leaving the dead body of my husband. I asked him if he wanted any wrap, and if he was feeling cold, I could spread it over him. He asked for water, but water could not be procured at that place.

I saw other people at the Bagh in search of their relatives. I passed my whole night there. It is impossible for me to describe what I felt. Heaps of dead bodies lay there, some on their backs and some with their faces upturned. A number of them were poor innocent children. I shall never forget the sight. I was all alone the whole night in that solitary jungle. Nothing but the barking of dogs, or the braying of donkeys was audible. Amidst hundreds of corpses, I passed my night, crying and watching. I cannot say more. What I experienced that night is known to me and to God. ❜

A LOCAL RESIDENT, RATAN DEVI, RECOUNTED HER HARROWING EXPERIENCE WAITING BY THE SIDE OF HER HUSBAND'S BODY.

‛Amritsar had behaved very badly and I think most of the inhabitants of Amritsar either gave assistance or were only waiting to see what was going to happen apparently. At any rate, they did not offer to help until after the firing; and if they suffered a little under martial law…’

THE INDISCRIMINATE LOGIC OF MARTIAL LAW, AS EXPLAINED BY DYER.

MARTIAL LAW

The authorities adopted various devious methods to strike terror in the hearts of the people. All the lawyers of the town were made special constables, insulted and abused, and made to witness public flogging and to carry furniture like ordinary coolies. All persons in the city were made to salam every Englishman. Disobedience to this resulted in arrest and detention in the lock up. Some were ordered to stand in the sun for hours in the hot season, and others made to learn salaaming by practicing it for some time. Handcuffing of respectable persons was the order of the day.

GIRDHARI LAL DESCRIBED THE PUNITIVE REGIME IMPLEMENTED UNDER MARTIAL LAW IN THE AFTERMATH OF THE MASSACRE.

'Two armed constables … began to beat me without saying anything. They beat me till I passed urine. Then they caused my trousers to be put off, and beat me severely with shoes and a cane. I cried out, and asked what they wanted from me. Upon this, I was abused and beaten again, and asked to become "All right." I told them I did not understand what they wanted.… The Sub-Inspector shook me by the beard, and said that I must name Saif-uddin Kitchlew, Bashir, Dr Satyapal and Badrul Islam and others, if I wanted to be released. I said, I was not acquainted with any one of these persons, although I had known some of them by sight. At this, they beat me again, till I became senseless.'

GHOLAM JILANI, A LOCAL IMAM, SURVIVED THE MASSACRE ON 13 APRIL, BUT WAS SUBSEQUENTLY ARRESTED BY THE POLICE.

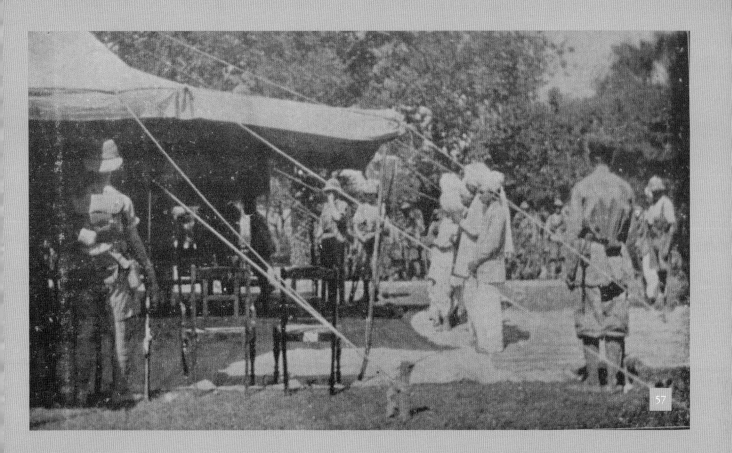

55 A prisoner being flogged at Ram Bagh garden in Amritsar. This was one of several secretly recorded photographs that were smuggled out of India in 1919 by Benjamin Horniman. A British journalist and editor of *The Bombay Chronicle*, Horniman broke the story about the massacre and its aftermath in the *Daily Herald*.

56 A prisoner under armed guard at Ram Bagh garden.

57 A summary court under martial law.

58 'A lesson in salaaming': local residents being 'taught' to show resepct to Europeans.

❝The reluctance of the people of Amritsar City to give information which would lead to the arrest and punishments of conspirators and rioters was very noticeable indeed, and if doubtful methods were used to obtain evidence or if prosecution by the police took place, the inhabitants of Amritsar themselves are more to blame than anyone else. They did not render the assistance which it was their bounden duty to give and their attitude only made the procuring of definite evidence as to the existence of corruption an impossibility but was in my opinion the primary cause and principal incentive to any corruption or persecution that may have taken place.❞

ACCORDING TO PROVOST MARSHAL, MAJOR
S. R. SHIRLEY, THE POPULATION OF AMRITSAR
WERE THEMSELVES TO BLAME FOR THE POLICE
CORRUPTION AND ABUSE OF POWER DURING
MARTIAL LAW.

59 A public flogging of a prisoner at Kasur
    railway station during martial law in Punjab.

60

I must say, however, that the pride which I myself, and my countrymen felt in British justice has received a rude shock. None of us could ever have thought that what happened during the Martial Law period was possible anywhere within the British Empire. Much of the ideal, which we cherished of British justice and beneficence, has been, I regret to have to say, shattered. So far as the people of Amritsar are concerned, I pray to god that we may not have to see those Martial Law days again.

ONE RESIDENT OF AMRITSAR, MIAN FEROZ DIN, DESCRIBED THE IMPACT OF LIVING UNDER MARTIAL LAW.

60 British officials inspecting prisoners during martial law in Punjab.

61 The result of mass-arrests in Punjab.

62 The erection of gallows at Kasur to terrorise the local population.

A helpless woman had been mercilessly beaten, in a most cruel manner, by a lot of dastardly cowards. She was beaten with sticks and shoes, and knocked down six times in the street. She tried to get entrance at an open door, but the door was slammed in her face. To be beaten with shoes is considered by Indians to be the greatest insult. It seemed intolerable to me that some suitable punishment could not be meted out. Civil law was at an end and I searched my brain for some military punishment to meet the case.

THE RATIONALE BEHIND DYER'S ORDER FOR INDIANS TO CRAWL ALONG THE STREET WHERE MISS SHERWOOD HAD BEEN ATTACKED.

While I was groping my way into the street with the support of a stick that I always carry, I was asked by a policeman to halt. On my begging of him to let me proceed, I was told that I could only do so if I was willing to crawl over the whole length. I informed the policeman that I had been practically starving for the last two days, but he would not let me go. I then had to crawl on my belly, and had hardly gone a few yards when I received a kick on my back, and my stick slipped off my hands. I then moved on, begging for alms from the residents of the quarter, but was advised to leave the place as owing to the bad times through which they were passing, the residents were not in a position to give me food. I then with great difficulty managed to make my way out of the lane by the side of Kaurianwala well.

THE ELDERLY BEGGAR, KAHAN CHAND, WAS ONE OF THE LOCALS WHO WERE FORCED TO CRAWL BY THE BRITISH SOLDIERS.

63 The enforcement of the crawling order in Kucha Kaurianwala, the 'crawling lane'.

64

64 A picket of soldiers from the 25th
London Cyclists who enforced the
crawling order in April 1919.

65 Soldier standing next to the flogging
post in the 'crawling lane'. On the back
of this photograph, the photographer,
Sergeant Reginald Howgego, wrote a
blatant lie: 'Set up as a deterrent. I did
not see or hear of it actually in use.'

'Sundar Singh was the first to be fastened to the flogging post (*tiktiki*) and given 30 stripes. He became senseless after the 4th stripe, but when some water was poured into his mouth by a soldier, he regained consciousness; he was again subjected to flogging. He lost his consciousness for the second time, but the flogging never ceased till he was given thirty stripes. He was taken off the flogging post, bleeding and quite unconscious. Mela was the second to be tied to the post. He too became unconscious after receiving four of five stripes. He was given some water, and the flogging continued. Magtu was the third victim. He too got thirty stripes. While Mangtu was being flogged, I cried bitterly and I could bear the sight no longer.... I saw the six boys who had just received flogging, bleeding badly. They were all handcuffed, and, as they could not walk even a few paces, they were dragged away by the Police. They were taken to the Fort.'

A LOCAL RESIDENT, PANDIT SALIG RAM, DESCRIBED THE FLOGGING HE WITNESSED IN THE CRAWLING LANE, KUCHA KAURIANWALA.

'The chances were from what I had heard and been told that these were the particular men. If they were not the particular men and another man was beaten, still it did not matter very much whether he was beaten there or somewhere else, if he was convicted. I did not wish to run the risk, if he had committed the offence against Miss Sherwood, of his being beaten somewhere else; therefore when I heard that these were the men, I had them beaten in the same street.'

WHETHER THE YOUNG MEN BEING FLOGGED WERE GUILTY OR NOT WAS, IN DYER'S ESTIMATION, LESS IMPORTANT THAN THE NEED TO SET AN EXAMPLE IN THE CRAWLING LANE.

66 A British soldier with fixed bayonet watches on as a prisoner is publically flogged in Punjab during April 1919.

"I saw many people passing through that lane being made to crawl on their bellies, and I also saw the British soldiers taking photographs of those who were made to crawl in that way."

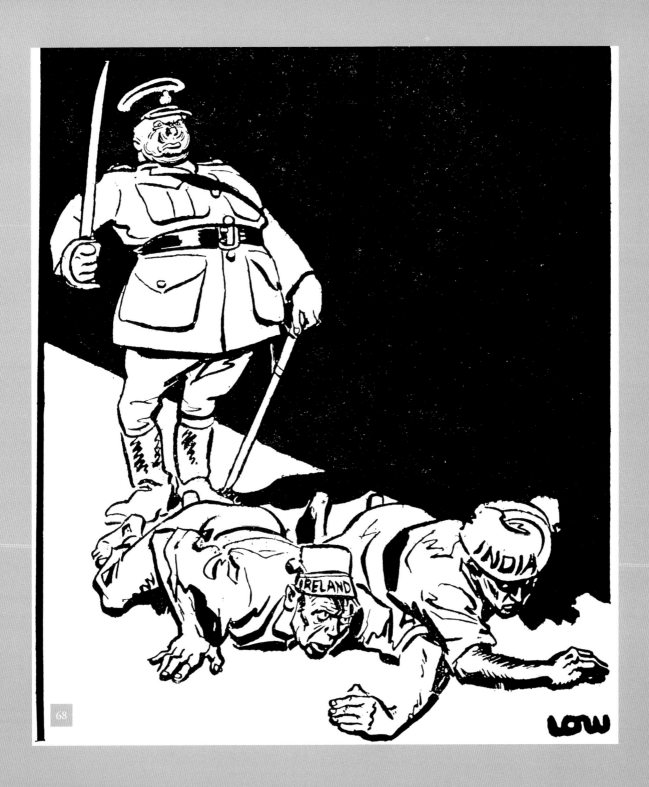

67 Soldiers of the 25th London Cyclists enforcing the crawling order at the point of a bayonet.

68 The snapshot of soldiers in the crawling lane was used as inspiration for this cartoon by David Low. Entitled 'Progress to Liberty – Amritsar Style' and published in *The Daily News* in December 1919, it depicts a Prussian-looking British officer terrorising both India and Ireland.

70

69, 70 Later re-enactments of the crawling
order in Kucha Kaurianwala.

❛ [This] is an episode which appears to me to be without precedent or parallel in the modern history of the British Empire. It is an event of an entirely different order from any of those tragical occurrences which take place when troops are brought into collision with the civil population. It is an extraordinary event, a monstrous event, an event which stands in singular and sinister isolation. ❜

WINSTON CHURCHILL ADDRESSING THE HOUSE OF COMMONS ON
8 JULY 1920.

AFTERMATH

We're in a bit of a mess out here. Racial hatred in towns leaping in a twink [ie instant] to pillage and murder, murder too of the most horrible kind. Then panic and cruelty – the two go together. I understand now why Germans did those terrible things in Belgium, they got cold feet passing through and fell blindly upon the people whom they feared. We did not rape or hack to pieces, but one day in Amritsar they shot down hundreds, mostly zemindars [ie villagers], there by religious hazard (Bhaisakh Day). I have seen the place – a death-trap. 5 or 6,000 there, the kernel of them thoroughly seditious, but the majority lookers on, mooching about as zemindars do. Enter infuriated general – "I took thirty seconds to make up my mind", said he to Wathen – and then – 1500 rounds. God it makes me sick to think of it. Yet I was told by my chief ten days later – "people at the Club (Lahore) say you ought to be court martialled for criticising".

MALCOLM DARLING OF THE INDIAN CIVIL SERVICE DESCRIBED THE SITUATION IN A LETTER TO HIS CLOSE FRIEND, E. M. FORSTER.

The order went out that no meetings were to be held. The blackguard leaders told the mob we should never dare to fire, so a huge meeting collected. They got their desserts this time, for the troops were ready, and fired and killed over 200, and a good thing too.… Fear is the only thing by which you can rule a wild uneducated crowd, and thank heaven Sir Michael [O'Dwyer] and General Dyer acted as they did. I don't care what Gerard [her husband] says, or any of those other sentimentalists. That shooting was drastic, but it was needed, and it's done more good than a hundred years of soft talk and reasoning – and I *believe* it will carry more weight than all the subtle lies and reasonings of these seditionists – for the people have learnt that after certain limits we do at last turn, and *hurt*, and that is a fact…

AN ANGLO-INDIAN WOMAN, MELICENT WATHEN, WHO EXPERIENCED THE DISTURBANCES FIRST-HAND, HAD LITTLE SYMPATHY FOR THE PEOPLE OF AMRITSAR.

"Sahib," they said, "you must become a Sikh even as Nikalseyn Sahib became a Sikh." The General thanked them for the honour, but he objected that he could not as a British officer let his hair grow long. Arur Singh laughed. "We will let you off the long hair," he said. General Dyer offered another objection, "But I cannot give up smoking."

"That you must do," said Arur Singh.

"No," said the General, "I am very sorry, but I cannot give up smoking."

The priest conceded, "We will let you give it up gradually."

"That I promise you," said the General, "at the rate of one cigarette a year."

The Sikhs, chuckling, proceeded with the initiation. General Dyer and Captain Briggs were invested with the five *kakas*, the sacred emblems of that war-like brotherhood, and so became Sikhs. Moreover, a shrine was built to General Dyer at their holy place, Guru Sat Sultani [Gurusar Satlani], and when a few days afterwards came the news that the Afghans were making war upon India, the Sikh leaders offered the General ten thousand men to fight for the British Raj if only he would consent to command them.

BEFORE HIS DEPARTURE BACK TO BRITAIN, DYER WAS INVITED TO THE GOLDEN TEMPLE BY ITS MANAGER TO BECOME AN 'HONORARY SIKH', AS DESCRIBED IN THE POSTHUMOUSLY PUBLISHED BIOGRAPHY BY IAN COLVIN.

71 Arur Singh, the manager of the Harimandir Sahib, made Dyer an honorary Sikh soon after the massacre.

'The enormity of the measures taken by the Government in the Punjab for quelling some local disturbances has, with a rude shock, revealed to our minds the helplessness of our position as British subjects in India.... The accounts of the insults and sufferings by our brothers in Punjab have trickled through the gagged silence, reaching every corner of India, and the universal agony of indignation roused in the hearts of our people has been ignored by our rulers – possibly congratulating themselves for what they imagine as salutary lessons. This callousness has been praised by most of the Anglo-Indian papers, which have in some cases gone to the brutal length of making fun of our sufferings, without receiving the least check from the same authority – relentlessly careful in smothering every cry of pain and expression of judgement from the organs representing the sufferers. Knowing that our appeals have been in vain ... the very least that I can do for my country is to take all consequences upon myself in giving voice to the protest of the millions of my countrymen, surprised into a dumb anguish of terror. The time has come when badges of honour make our shame glaring in their incongruous context of humiliation, and I for my part wish to stand shorn of all special distinctions...'

ON 31 MAY 1919, THE BENGALI POET AND NOBEL PRIZE LAUREATE, RABINDRANATH TAGORE, WROTE TO THE VICEROY, LORD CHELMSFORD, TO FORMALLY RENOUNCE HIS KNIGHTHOOD IN PROTEST AGAINST BRITISH OPPRESSION IN PUNJAB.

72 Rabindranath Tagore

' Pandits Malaviya and [Motilal] Nehru accompanied by others visited the Jallianwala Bagh again … and took the photos of the holes caused by the bullets in the walls of the houses surrounding the Bagh. The people are still coming to them in great numbers, and tell all sorts of exaggerated stories, which are generally accepted as true. '

A CID REPORT DESCRIBED THE CONGRESS LEADERS' VISIT TO THE SITE OF THE MASSACRE IN LATE AUGUST 1919.

' I have been twice to the Jallianwala Bagh. The walls around it still speak of the murders that were committed there, of the volleys of service bullets that were fired at the people who were assembled at a meeting, who had no arms, who were not making any protest against anything, but were sitting down to hear a lecture. According to the official statement made yesterday, 300 of such men were massacred there. Perhaps, when the inquiry proceeds further, it will be found that the popular estimate that over 1,000 were killed is nearer the truth. '

HAVING INVESTIGATED THE EVENTS AT AMRITSAR, MADAN MOHAN MALAVIYA GAVE A SPEECH IN THE LEGISLATIVE COUNCIL ON 12 SEPTEMBER 1919.

73 Madan Mohan Malaviya

74 The scars of the massacre: bullet-holes,
some six inches deep, in the western wall
of the Jallianwala Bagh.

74

AFTERMATH | 139

75 Local residents showing the bullet-holes in
the southern wall towards the western side.

76 A man pointing out a bullet-hole in the southern wall, which is covered in anti-
British graffiti. One Hindi couplet reads: 'Hindu and Muslim brothers came to
listen to a lecture, [but] Dyer the coward came and made a river of blood.'

'The massacre of Glenco in English history is no greater a blot on the fair name of my country than the massacre at Amritsar. I am not speaking from idle rumour. I have gone into every single detail with all the care and thoroughness (that a personal investigation could command) and it remains to me an unspeakable disgrace, indefensible, unpardonable, inexcusable. And I am obliged to go on from that incident to what followed under Martial Law. I have seen with my own eyes the very men who have endured the crawling order, the compulsion to grovel on their bellies in the dust, the public flogging which was administered to hundreds of men and hundred other desecrations of man's image which according to our Christian scriptures is made in the likeness of God. This ruthless and deliberate emasculation of manhood by the brute force of the military and the police appears to me no less an indelible stain on the fair honour of my country than the massacre at Jallianwala Bagh itself. These are the very few words which I have felt compelled as an Englishman to say with regard to the culminating acts of the Disturbance. Every day that I have been working side by side with my Indian fellow-workers, the deep sense of the wrong done has come home to me, and each act has been in very truth an act of penance, of atonement, an act of reparation for my country.'

THE CHRISTIAN EDUCATOR AND SOCIAL REFORMER, CHARLES FREER ANDREWS,
WHO HAD TAKEN PART IN THE UNOFFICIAL INQUIRY INTO THE MASSACRE AND ITS
AFTERMATH IN AMRITSAR, GAVE HIS FAREWELL SPEECH AT LAHORE IN NOVEMBER 1919.

77 Charles Freer Andrews

78

79

80

81

❝ As desired in the official notification, I give below a brief account of the tragic death of my son, Madan Mohan, which occurred in the Jallianwala Bagh on the 13th April last. The delay in submitting this information is due to my absence from Amritsar to Mussoorie hills. Jallianwala Bagh is at a distance of about three minutes' walk and is the only open place near my house which is opposite the Clock Tower. My son, Madan Mohan, aged about 13 years … along with his playmates used to visit this open square for play almost daily. On the 13th April last he went there as usual and met his tragic end, having been shot in the head which fractured his skull, he bled and died instantaneously. I with eight or nine others had to search for about half an hour till I could pick up his corpse as it was mixed up with hundreds of dead bodies lying in heaps there, who met their respective ends under circumstances well known. This is how my innocent child of innocent age was murdered by those who allege they acted in the name of justice, law and order. ❞

WHEN THE BRITISH AUTHORITIES CALLED FOR THE RESIDENTS OF AMRITSAR TO SUBMIT THE NAMES OF RELATIVES KILLED AT JALLIANWALA BAGH, DR MANI RAM, A DENTAL SURGEON, WAS AMONG THE RESPONDENTS. HE WAS EVENTUALLY AWARDED 8,362 RUPEES IN COMPENSATION FOR THE LOSS OF HIS SON.

78 The twelve-year-old Madan Mohan, who was killed at Jallianwala Bagh on 13 April.

79 Sundar Singh, who lost an eye in the shooting.

80 Uttam Chand, who lost a leg after being wounded by Dyer's troops.

81 Mangal Singh, who lost the use of his right arm after being shot.

No.	Name of person killed with parentage, age and residence.	Occupation.	Name of d
65	Madan Mohan, son of Dr. Mani Ram, Khatri, 12 years, Bazar Ghantaghar.	Student ...	Father Mani Ram, 41 years ; brother Dhani Kishendo, 5 years ; brot mother, 33 years ; sister
66	Murli Mal, son of Labu Mal, Arora, 60 years, Kucha Ram Nand, Katra Ahluwalian.	Mistri, shopkeeper	Son Natha Singh, 20 yea years ; widow Prem Kau
67	Sohan Lal, alias Ram Nath, son of Dasu Mal, Khatri, 8 years, Kucha Dhrel, Katra, Ahlu-walian.	Student ...	Father Dasu Mal, Dalal, Thakar Devi ; brother A Jaghindar, 4 years ; br sister Silo.
68	Hira Nand, son of Mehraj Mal, Arora, 40 years, (Ajnala), Katra Bhangian, Amritsar.	Petition-writer	Son Tek Chand, 20 years son Diwan Chand, 13 Devi, 4 years.
69	Ismail, son of Miran Bakhsh, Zargar, 32 years, Kucha Asadulla, Katra Jaimal Singh.	Goldsmith ...	Widow Ghulam Fatima, Alam, 13 years ; son Ab son Fazil Hussain, 4 Begum, 6 years.
70	Nur Mohd., Muazin Masjid Khalil, Katra Ahluwalian, 25 years.	Muazan and Daryai weaving.	Son Ghulam Kadir, 7 yea

82 Extract from the list of victims for whom compensation was paid by the British Government. Madan Mohan is no. 65.

	Annual income of the deceased.	RECOMMENDATIONS OF THE COMMITTEE.			REMARKS.
.		Capitalized value.	Proportion assigned	Amount recommended.	
	Rs.	Rs.		Rs.	
ter Des Raj, 21 years; brother arkash, 3 years; 10 years.	...	16,725	1/2	8,362	Payable to father.
Sant Singh, 14 ars.	1,000	9,877	4/5	7,901	1/3 to widow. 1/3 to each son (minor's share to be invested).
cloth; mother year; brother nak, 2½ years;	...	16,725	1/2	8,362	Payable to father.
m Pal, 16 years; daughter Maya	1,200	18,800	4/5	15,040	1/7 to daughter. 2/7 to each son. (Share of 2 minor sons and 1 daughter to be invested).
son Khurshaid ssain, 10 years; laughter Wazir	700	12,064	4/5	9,651	1/9 to daughter 2/9 to each son } To be invested. 2/9 to widow.
... ...	300	5,525	2/3	3,683	To son (to be invested).

82

General Dyer wanted by his action at Jallianwala Bagh to create a "wide impression" and "a great moral effect." We have no doubt that he did succeed in creating a very wide impression and a great moral effect, but of a character quite opposite to the one he intended. The story of this indiscriminate killing of innocent people not engaged in committing any acts of violence, but assembled in a meeting, has undoubtedly produced such a deep impression throughout the length and breadth of the country, so prejudicial to the British Government that it would take a good deal and a long time to rub it out. The action of General Dyer, as well as some acts of the martial law administration … have been compared to the acts of "frightfulness" committed by some of the German military commanders during the war in Belgium and France.

It is pleaded that General Dyer honestly believed that what he was doing was right. This cannot avail him, if he was clearly wrong in his notions of what was right and what was wrong; and the plea of military necessity is the plea that has always been advanced in justification of the Prussian atrocities. General Dyer thought that he had crushed the rebellion, and Sir Michael O'Dwyer was of the same view. There was no rebellion which required to be crushed. We feel that General Dyer, by adopting an inhuman and un-British method of dealing with subjects of His Majesty the King-Emperor, has done great disservice to the interest of British rule in India. This aspect it was not possible for the people of the mentality of General Dyer to realise.

THE MINORITY REPORT, WRITTEN BY THE INDIAN MEMBERS OF THE HUNTER COMMITTEE, CONDEMNED DYER AND THE BRITISH SUPPRESSION OF THE UNREST IN PUNJAB IN NO UNCERTAIN TERMS.

Sir, I am commanded to inform you that the Army Council have considered the report of the Hunter Committee … I am to say that the Council consider that, in spite of the great difficulties of the position in which you found yourself on 13 April, 1919, at Jallianwalah Bagh, you cannot be acquitted of an error of judgment. They observe that the Commander-in-Chief in India has removed you from his employment, that you have been informed that no further employment will be offered you in India, that you have in consequence reverted to half pay, and that the Selection Board in India have passed you over for promotion. These decisions the Army Council accept. They do not consider that further employment should be offered to you outside India. They have also considered whether any further action of a disciplinary nature is required from them; but in view of all the circumstances they do not feel called upon, from the military point of view with which they are alone concerned, to take any further action.

I am, Sir, Your obedient Servant,

H. J. Creedy

THE LETTER FROM THE WAR OFFICE INFORMING DYER THAT HE WOULD NO LONGER FIND EMPLOYMENT IN THE ARMY.

' I shot to save the British Raj – to preserve India for the Empire, and to protect Englishmen and Englishwomen who looked to me for protection. And now I am told to go for doing my duty – my horrible, dirty duty.… I had to shoot. I had 30 seconds to make up my mind what action to take, and I did it. Every Englishman I have met in India has approved my act, horrible as it was. What should have happened if I had not shot? I and my little force would have been swept away like chaff, and then what would have happened?… If I had done anything wrong I should be court-martialled, but there has been no suggestion of that. I have never been heard in my own defence. '

EXTRACT FROM DYER'S INTERVIEW IN THE *DAILY MAIL*, 5 MAY 1920, THE DAY HE ARRIVED BACK IN BRITAIN.

83 General Dyer as he disembarked at Portsmouth on 4 May 1920.

Overleaf:

84, 85 Coverage of the Dyer debate on 8 July 1920 in the House of Commons, as reported in *The Illustrated London News*, 17 July 1920.

THE AMRITSAR DEBATE: HIGH OFFICIALS CONCERNED IN THE CASE.

PHOTOGRAPHS SUPPLIED BY C.N., VANDYK, RUSSELL, AND DRUMMOND-YOUNG.

THE SECRETARY OF STATE FOR INDIA: THE RT. HON. E. S. MONTAGU, WHO SPOKE ON AMRITSAR ON JULY 8.

THE VICEROY OF INDIA: LORD CHELMSFORD.

THE LIEUTENANT-GOVERNOR OF THE PUNJAB, WHO APPROVED OF GENERAL DYER'S ACTION: SIR MICHAEL O'DWYER.

CHAIRMAN OF THE COMMITTEE APPOINTED TO REPORT ON THE AMRITSAR DISTURBANCES: LORD HUNTER.

EXTRACT FROM MR. MONTAGU'S SPEECH.
("Times" Report.)

"ARE you going to hold India by terrorism, racial humilation, and subordination, and frightfulness, or rest it upon the good-will of the people of your Indian Empire? It is no use one Session passing a great Act of Parliament on the principle of partnership for India, and then allowing your administration to depend on terrorism. That is one choice. There is the other, to hold India by the sword, to recognise terrorism, to guard British honour and British life with callousness about Indian honour and Indian life. . . . There has been no criticism of any officer, however drastic his action was, in any province outside the Punjab. There were 37 instances of firing during the terrible, dangerous disturbances of last year. The Government have only censured one, because, however good the motive, it infringed the principle which has always animated the British Army and the principles upon which our Indian Empire has been built. . . . The great objection to terrorism is that, having once tried it, you must go on. There is no end to it, until the people rise."

Mr. Montagu's speech in the House of Commons on July 8 on the action of General Dyer at Amritsar aroused many expressions of disapproval. Mr. Montagu has been Secretary of State for India since 1917. Lord Chelmsford has been Viceroy of India since 1916. Sir Michael O'Dwyer has been Lieutenant-Governor of the Punjab since 1913. He was commended in the Hunter Committee's Report for "energy, decision and courage," but the Indian Government considered his approval of General Dyer's action premature. Lord Hunter is Senator of the College of Justice in Scotland, and was formerly Solicitor-General for Scotland.

EXTRACT FROM MR. CHURCHILL'S SPEECH.
("Times" Report.)

"AT the Jallianwalla Bagh the crowd was not armed, except with bludgeons, and it was not attacking anybody or anything. It was penned up in a space smaller than Trafalgar Square. The people ran madly this way and that, and the firing was only stopped when the ammunition was on the point of exhaustion. When 379 persons had been killed, the troops, at whom not even a stone had been thrown, marched away. He did not think it was in the interests of the British Empire or Army for us to take a load of that sort for all time upon our back. We had to make it absolutely clear that that was not the British way of doing things. . . . His personal opinion was that the conduct of General Dyer deserved to be marked by a definite disciplinary act. It was quite true that his conduct had been approved by superiors and that events had taken place which amounted to virtual condonation. General Dyer might have done wrong, but he had his rights, and he did not see how, in face of such virtual condonation, it would have been possible or right to take disciplinary action against him."

EXTRACT FROM GEN. DYER'S STATEMENT
("Times" Report.)

"I TOOK the small force at my disposal . . . and . . . arrived about 5 p.m. in the Jallianwalla Bagh. . . . I found a large meeting, afterwards ascertained to be from 15,000 to 20,000 in number, being addressed by a speaker engaged in violent exhortations . . . There were no women and children. . . . Hesitation I felt would be dangerous and futile, and as soon as my fifty riflemen had deployed I ordered fire to be opened. . . . When 1650 rounds or thereabouts had been fired . . . the whole crowd had dispersed. . . . I cannot understand how it can be suggested that the objects of crushing the rebellion, of diminishing the dangers in Lahore by 60 per cent., were not proper objects upon which to employ a military force. . . . I knew that, if I shirked . . . there would infallibly follow a general mob movement which would have destroyed all the European population. . . . I knew that I could produce no sufficient effect except by continuous firing."

EXTRACT FROM SIR W. JOYNSON-HICKS' SPEECH
("Times" Report.)

"HE (Sir W. Joynson-Hicks) had just returned from a visit to India and to Amritsar, and the opinions he was expressing were held by at least 80 per cent. of the Indian Civil Service throughout India and by 90 per cent. of the European people. . . . The General in charge at Lahore considered the quieting of Lahore was due as to 60 per cent. to the action of General Dyer at Amritsar. . . . General Dyer was faced with a rebellion. . . . He had talked to men on the spot, both native and English, and native officials supported General Dyer to the utmost, and they all testified that the inhabitants knew of the proclamations and the danger they would incur if they did not heed them. . . . When it was all over, was General Dyer assailed by the people? Not at all; they came in their thousands and thanked him. He was made a Sikh, and was employed to march round the whole district, and to pacify it—this bloodthirsty man! And let there be no mistake about it—General Dyer was beloved by the whole of the Sikh nation. . . . He (the speaker) insisted that the right thing to do was to trust the men on the spot."

BRIG.-GENERAL R.E.H. DYER, WHOSE ACTION AT AMRITSAR WAS DEBATED IN THE HOUSE OF COMMONS ON JULY 8.

Brigadier-General Dyer's action in firing on the mob at Amritsar, in April 1919, is said to be considered by the majority of Anglo-Indians to have prevented a rebellion, and to have saved all the European women in India from horrors equal to those of the Mutiny. One of the most acrimonious debates ever held in the House of Commons took place on July 8, following the announcement (made there on the previous day) that the Army Council had approved the decision that General Dyer should be removed from his employment, passed over for promotion, and placed on half-pay. The question was debated in committee by the House of Commons on the Vote for contributions towards the cost of the India Office. General Dyer was present in the gallery. Notable speeches were made both for and against him. His supporters included Sir Edward Carson, General Hunter-Weston, and Sir W. Joynson-Hicks. Against him were Mr. Montagu, Mr. Churchill, and Mr. Asquith. A Labour amendment to reduce the Vote by £100 was rejected by 247 votes to 37, and a similar amendment moved by Sir Edward Carson was rejected by 230 votes to 129.

'No more distasteful or responsible duty falls to the lot of the soldier than that which he is sometimes required to discharge in aid of the civil power. If his measures are too mild he fails in his duty. If they are deemed to be excessive he is liable to be attacked as a cold-blooded murderer. His position is one demanding the highest degree of sympathy from all reasonable and right-minded citizens. He is frequently called upon to act on the spur of the moment in grave situations in which he intervenes because all the other resources of civilisation have failed. His actions are liable to be judged by ex post facto standards, and by persons who are in complete ignorance of the realities which he had to face. His good faith is liable to be impugned by the very persons connected with the organisation of the disorders which his action has foiled. There are those who will admit that a measure of force may have been necessary, but who cannot agree with the extent of the force employed. How can they be in a better position to judge of that than the officer on the spot? It must be remembered that when a rebellion has been started against the Government, it is tantamount to a declaration of war. War cannot be conducted in accordance with standards of humanity to which we are accustomed in peace. Should not officers and men, who through no choice of their own, are called upon to discharge these distasteful duties, be in all fairness accorded that support which has been promised to them?'

LIEUTENANT-GENERAL SIR HAVELOCK HUDSON'S DEFENCE OF DYER QUOTED IN THE HOUSE OF COMMONS ON 8 JULY 1920.

"I want to suggest that Amritsar is not an isolated event any more than General Dyer is an isolated officer. These are not things that can be judged apart, if they resulted from a certain policy that some men have pursued, from a certain mentality that some men seem to possess in India in a most extraordinary degree. Talking about the curious mentality of some Anglo-Indians, may I be permitted to quote one short paragraph from the evidence of the Brigadier-General commanding the Delhi Brigade? It is taken from volume one, page 172 of the evidence: "Composed, as the crowd was, of the scum of Delhi, I am of opinion that if they had got a bit more firing given them it would have done them a world of good, and their attitude would be much more amenable and respectful, as force is the only thing that an Asiatic has any respect for." "

DURING THE HOUSE OF COMMONS DEBATE ON 8 JULY, LABOUR MP, BENJAMIN SPOOR, CRITICISED NOT JUST DYER BUT THE BROADER COLONIAL MENTALITY OF THE BRITISH MILITARY IN INDIA.

Overleaf:

86 Dyer's case being debated in the House of Lords on 19 July 1920.

87 Dyer with his wife and son on their way to the House of Lords.

THE ILLUSTRATED LONDON NEWS

REGISTERED AS A NEWSPAPER FOR TRANSMISSION IN THE UNITED KINGDOM AND TO CANADA AND NEWFOUNDLAND BY MAGAZINE POST.

No. 4240.—VOL. CLVII.   SATURDAY, JULY 24, 1920.   ONE SHILLING

The Copyright of all the Editorial Matter, both Engravings and Letterpress, is Strictly Reserved in Great Britain, the Colonies, Europe, and the United States of America.

GENERAL DYER'S CASE DEBATED IN THE HOUSE OF LORDS: THE LORD CHANCELLOR SPEAKING.

The House of Lords' debate on the punishment of General Dyer for his action at Amritsar began on July 19, when Viscount Finlay moved " That this House deplores the conduct of the case of General Dyer as unjust to that officer, and as establishing a precedent dangerous to the preservation of order in face of rebellion." Lord Finlay, in a very telling vindication of General Dyer, said : " He found a clear conviction that an organised movement was in progress to submerge and destroy all the Europeans on the spot and to carry the movement throughout the Punjab. . . . Thanks were showered on General Dyer from all quarters of India. He received hundreds of letters from natives thanking him for what he had done." The Earl of Midleton and Lord Ampthill also spoke in General Dyer's favour, while against him were the Lord Chancellor (Lord Birkenhead) and Lord Sinha. The debate was adjourned to the 20th.

DRAWN BY OUR SPECIAL ARTIST, STEVEN SPURRIER, R.O.I. COPYRIGHTED IN THE UNITED STATES AND CANADA.

GENERAL DYER GOING TO THE LORDS

General Dyer leaving, with Mrs. Dyer and his son, for the House, which carried a motion upholding the General by 129 votes to 86. By 230 votes to 129 the House of Commons had previously taken the opposite view of the General's conduct in connection with the tragedy at the Jallianwallah Bagh. 87

While General Dyer saved India, the politicians are saving themselves at his expense. It is a burning reproach to the British nation that such a thing should be possible. But the politicians have the power; and the only appeal is to the generous instincts of the people. In spite of the specious gloss put upon the case by those who, while reaping the benefit of General Dyer's action, find it convenient to escape the responsibility for it, there are thousands of men and women in England who realise the truth – that the lives of their fellow-country-men in India hung upon the readiness of a General Dyer to act as he acted. It is to those men and women that we appeal, to do what is in them to redress the callous and cynical wrong which has been done. General Dyer has been broken.

THE LAUNCH OF 'AN APPEAL TO PATRIOTS' FOR FUNDS FOR THE BENEFIT OF DYER BY THE RIGHT-WING NEWSPAPER *MORNING POST* ON 8 JULY 1920. DYER WAS LAUDED AS 'THE MAN WHO SAVED INDIA' AND ULTIMATELY RECEIVED MORE THAN £26,000.

The Army Council has found General Dyer guilty of error of judgment and advised that he should not receive any office under the Crown. Mr. Montagu has been unsparing in his criticism of General Dyer's conduct. And yet somehow or other I cannot help feeling that General Dyer is by no means the worst offender. His brutality is unmistakable. His abject and unsoldier-like cowardice is apparent in every line of his amazing defence before the Army Council. He has called an unarmed crowd of men and children – mostly holiday-makers – "a rebel army". He believes himself to be the saviour of the Punjab in that he was able to shoot down like rabbits men who were penned in an enclosure. Such a man is unworthy of being considered a soldier. There was no bravery in his action. He ran no risk. He shot without the slightest opposition and without warning. This is not an "error of judgment". It is paralysis of it in the face of fancied danger. It is proof of criminal incapacity and heartlessness. But the fury that has been spent upon General Dyer is, I am sure, largely misdirected. No doubt the shooting was "frightful", the loss of innocent life deplorable. But the slow torture, degradation and emasculation that followed was much worse, more calculated, malicious and soul-killing, and the actors who performed the deeds deserve greater condemnation than General Dyer for the Jallianwala Bagh massacre. The latter merely destroyed a few bodies but the others tried to kill the soul of a nation.

MOHANDAS KARAMCHAND GANDHI ON THE TRUE IMPACT OF THE BRITISH VIOLENCE IN PUNJAB.

88 Dyer died eight years after the Amritsar Massacre. His funeral took place over two days beginning with a church service in Somerset on 27 July 1927. Dyer's coffin was covered with the flag that had flown over his Amritsar headquarters.

‘THE MAN WHO SAVED INDIA

DEATH OF GENERAL DYER AFTER FIVE YEARS' ILLNESS

ECHO OF AMRITSAR RIOTS

"MORNING POST" READERS' WONDERFUL THANKOFFERING

We regret to announce that Brigadier-General R. E. H. Dyer, whose courageous decision at a moment of dangerous crisis at Amritsar in 1919 gained for him, in spite of official censure, the title of "The Saviour of the Punjab," died on Saturday night at his home, St. Martin's, Long Ashton, near Bristol.

A victim of political expediency of the worst type, General Dyer was publicly "broken" after he had been actually promoted, and in spite of the approbation of his action by his civil superior, Sir Michael O'Dwyer.... World-wide public appreciation of General Dyer's action was strikingly manifested when, in response to an appeal issued by the "Morning Post," no less a sum than £26,000 was received. ’

EXTRACT FROM DYER'S OBITUARY IN THE *MORNING POST*, 28 JULY 1927.

89

89, 90 On 28 July, Dyer was given a full military funeral in London.
His body was placed on a gun carriage and borne in state past
the Guards Division memorial to the Church of St Martin-in-
the-Fields near Trafalgar Square.

‘ General Dyer's action was denounced in unsparing terms by two Imperialists but fair-minded British statesmen, Lords Curzon and Milner. Sir Michael O'Dwyer's statement that "everyone in India approved his action" ignores the entire Indian population, who were shocked and embittered almost to a man. I can safely say that no British action, during the whole course of our history in India, has struck a severer blow to Indian faith in British justice than the massacre at Amritsar, and the attitude of official Anglo-India towards it. ’

LETTER FROM A RETIRED BRITISH COLONIAL OFFICIAL, WRITING ANONYMOUSLY AS '47 YEARS IN INDIA', PUBLISHED IN THE *WESTMINSTER GAZETTE*, 27 JULY 1927.

91 News of the assassination of Sir Michael O'Dwyer at the hands of Udham Singh (aka 'Mahomed Singh Azad') hit the front pages of the British press.

DAILY MIRROR, Thursday, March 14, 1940.

Daily Mirror

MAR 14

No. 11,315   ONE PENNY
Registered at the G.P.O. as a Newspaper.

ASSASSIN SHOOTS MINISTER, KILLS KNIGHT

Thirty-seven-year-old Indian, Mahomed Singh Azad, leaving the Caxton Hall with police. He was charged last night with the murder of Sir Michael O'Dwyer and with wounding Lord Lamington, Sir Louis Dane and Lord Zetland by shooting them with a revolver.

SIR MICHAEL O'DWYER, AGED SEVENTY-FIVE, GOVERNOR OF THE PUNJAB DURING THE AMRITSAR RIOTS IN 1919, WAS SHOT DEAD BY AN INDIAN GUNMAN AT A CROWDED MEETING IN CAXTON HALL, WESTMINSTER, YESTERDAY.

The gunman fired first at Lord Zetland, Secretary of State for India, and slightly wounded him. Then, as they rose to reach him he turned his gun, shot and wounded Lord Lamington, aged seventy-nine, ex- Governor of Bombay, and Sir Louis Dane, aged eighty-four, another Punjab ex-Governor.

Nearly 300 men and women had heard Sir Percy Sykes address the meeting of the East India Association in the Tudor Room of Caxton Hall.

Lord Zetland was in the chair. The meeting was about to close and Lord Lamington had risen to propose a vote of thanks, when a thick-set Indian rose, walked to the Press table, pulled out a revolver and fired.

As the first two shots were fired Lord Zetland toppled over and collapsed on the arms of his chair.

Sir Michael O'Dwyer jumped up. Two shots entered his heart and he fell back dead.

Assassin Fired
Six Shots

The assassin fired six times. With his last two bullets he wounded Lord Lamington and Sir Louis Dane, who had been sitting at each end of the front row of the audience.

Sir Louis was hit in the arm; Lord Lamington's right hand was shattered.

For a shocked second no one moved. The assassin turned, shouted "Make way, make way," and dashed down the aisle.

Two men, one of them in uniform, jumped on a man and threw him. Then men and women jumped to their feet, shouted, "Murder, police a doctor."

A woman doctor, Dr. Grace **(Continued on Back Page)**

Lord Zetland—a bullet grazed his ribs, and he fell.

Lord Lamington was shot in the hand.

Sir Michael O'Dwyer—died with two bullet wounds in his heart.

FINN, SWEDE, NORWAY PACT

A CONFERENCE between Finland, Sweden and Norway for the conclusion of a treaty of defensive alliance will be opened immediately, declared M. Tanner, the Finnish Foreign Minister, in Helsinki last night.

M. Tanner stated that the war with Russia had prevented the investigation of the possibilities of such a pact, which he said "will secure the frontiers and the independence of these three nations."

Soviet-Rumanian Treaty

He added that it had been agreed by the Governments of the three countries that now a Russo-Finnish peace has been re-established, the question of an alliance should be investigated.

Plans for a non-aggression pact between Russia and Rumania were reported in Bukarest, Rumanian capital, last night to be under consideration. The talks would be held in Berlin.

A military commission composed of high-ranking Rumanian Army officials is at present in Berlin. The Rumanian delegation is reported to have left for Berlin secretly, says the Associated Press.
Sweden to Rebuild Finn Front—Page 3.

91

'The cold-blooded Amritsar Massacre did not fail to arouse fiery indignations among all other Asiatics for it was typical of the kind of cruelty and savagery dealt out by the hands of the British.… In all parts of Asia which has come under the stretching claws of ruthless British rule, repeated acts of similar nature have been committed against the Asiatics in untold numbers.'

FROM A JAPANESE PROPAGANDA POSTER PUBLISHED DURING THE SECOND WORLD WAR THAT GRAPHICALLY ILLUSTRATES THE MASSACRE.

PICTURING
THE MASSACRE

92 This is the first ever visual representation of the Amritsar Massacre. It was created by the artist Eduard Thöny for the German satirical magazine *Simplicissimus* in January 1920.

92

' Those men only understood the language of the stick and could not be talked to. When I kicked their backside, it brought me immense joy. Today, I have made them forget all the big talk. [During the firing] they were running here and there, trying to escape with fear in their hearts. Now, there will be no gatherings as they all got what they deserved. I have not given up yet, I will now kill more in the city. '

WORDS ASCRIBED TO DYER IN THE PLAY *JULMI DYER YA JALIYANVALA BAGH*. PUBLISHED IN 1922, IT RECOUNTS THE HISTORICAL INCIDENT FROM THE POINT OF VIEW OF A CHILD NAMED MOHAN MADAN WHO IS KILLED IN THE MASSACRE.

93 This front cover of the play *Julmi Dyer ya Jaliyanvala Bagh* ('Cruel Dyer and Jallianwala Bagh') written by Manohar Lal Shukla in 1922, is full of allegorical imagery. A policeman named 'Martial Law' holds a whip in one hand and the mantle of a lady named 'Afflicted Punjab'. He threatens to disrobe her while she prays to Lord Vishnu, an allusion to the story of Draupadi in the *Mahabharat*. The law books, labelled 'Vyavastha', lie unattended on the ground, while a male figure resembling Gandhi, named 'Satyagraha', sits in helpless contemplation.

ਜਲ੍ਹਿਆਂ ਵਾਲ੍ਹਾ ਬਾਗ

ਖਾਤਿਰ ਅਪਨੇ ਦੇਸ਼ ਦੀ
ਹੋਵਨ ਜੋ ਕੁਰਬਾਨ ।
ਮਰਦੇ ਨਹੀਂ ਉਹ ਜੀਊਂਦੇ
ਰੋਸ਼ਨ ਵਿਚ ਜਹਾਨ ।।
ਜਲ੍ਹਿਆਂ ਵਾਲੇ ਬਾਗ਼ ਵਿਚ
ਹੋਇਆ ਜ਼ੁਲਮ ਅਪਾਰ ।
ਹਿੰਦੂ ਮੁਸਲਮਾਨ ਸਿੱਖ
ਕਰਦੇ ਹਾ! ਹਾ!! ਕਾਰ

MARTYRS
OF
COUNTRY
OR
Jullianwala Bagh
INDIA'S MOTHER
Bharat Mata:—

Enough of that my sons
Never before had so much
sacrifice been evinced by
any body in the History
of the World as by you in
"Jullianwala Bagh"
Swaraj is thine. Behold
over there. That has
already been ordained
for thee.

وطن کی خاطر جو اپنی جان دیا کرتے ہیں
مرتے نہیں ہیں وہ ہمیشہ کیلئے جیا کرتے ہیں

یہ اب وہ پہلا سا جلیانوالا باغ نہیں
وطن پرستوں کا ہے یہ شوالہ باغ نہیں

94 An Indian poster from the early 1920s depicting the Jallianwala Bagh massacre as a British plane soars overhead. Titled 'Sacred Sight of Punjab's Heroes', it shows Mother India blessing the Hindu, Muslim and Sikh victims of the atrocity, and is framed with verses exalting their sacrifice. Also shown are portraits of key nationalist leaders, including Gandhi and Motilal Nehru, and of some of the victims. One of them, the only female, is Ratan Devi, who spent the harrowing night of the 13th tending to her husband's corpse.

95 German depiction of the Amritsar Massacre from 1939 under the headline 'One of the many disgraces of British colonial history: the bloodbath of Amritsar'. The accompanying caption describes how the 'English bloodhound General Dyer ... completely without reason opened fire'. Claiming that 1,200 were killed and 3,000 wounded as a result of 'this animal wickedness', it concludes: 'The "humane" general forbid that help be brought to the men, women and children rolling in their blood.'

96 The Hindi and Bangla text of this Second World War propaganda leaflet, which depicts an Indian woman holding her man in a sea of dead bodies, while in the background the Indian National Army is seen chasing fleeing British troops, reads:

Those Indians who still do not get agitated after remembering Amritsar incident are not Indians.

The time has now come to take unprecedented revenge.

97 The Hindi and Bangla text of this anti-British leaflet reads:

1765: Tyranny in Dhaka
1857: 1st war of Indian Independence

Glorious Freedom. Revenge for our blood-bathed history.

"India's main well-wisher and most understanding" white men have, for 300 years, created a defective system of confusion, bribery and murders, and whipped us. The time has come for us to realise our long-sought-after wish of independence. India has got the opportunity to take revenge for our blood-bathed history and get glorious freedom. Shall we lose such an opportunity by staying still and not doing anything?

1918: Sacrifice in First World War
1919: The Jallianwala Bagh episode of Amritsar

सन १७६५
সন ১৭৬৫
ढाका का अत्याचार
ঢাকাতে অত্যাচার
सन १८५७
সন ১৮৫৭
भारत-स्वतंत्रता का प्रथम युद्ध
ভারত স্বাধীনতার প্রথম যুদ্ধ
गौरवपूर्ण स्वाधीनता॥ खून के इतिहास का परिशोध
গৌরবময় স্বাধীনতা। অবিচ্ছিন্ন অত্যাচারের সমাপ্তি
सन १९१८
সন ১৯১৮
सन १९१९
সন ১৯১৯
अमृतसर का निर्मम हत्याकांड
অমৃতসরের নির্মম হত্যাকাণ্ড

97

REMEMBER THE AMRITSAR INCID

British brutality is the enemy of entire Asia, of all mankind.

アクマノ ヤウナ エイコクハ アジアノ テキデアル
ノミナラズ ゼンセカイノ テキデアル。

Souvenons-nous du grand massacre d'Amritsar! Les Anglais, ces bourreaux sans scrupule, sont ennemis de toute l'Asie, de toute l'humanité!

.မေ့ေလျာ့ကြပြီလား၊ အမ္ရလိဆ၊ ၏၊ အရေး၊ တော်ပုံကို—
လူ့တို့၏ တရား၊ လ၀်နေ ကြောင်း၊ ကိုမြင်၊ ၍ ဆက် တက် သေ၁၁ဘက် လိမ့်မည်.
မဟာ၁ရ၏၊ ရန်၊ သူကြီး၊ ပင် မြစ်၍၊ လူမျိုး၊ အား၊ လုံး၊ တို့၏ ရန်သူ ကြီး၊ ပ၊ ည်း
မြစ်ကေ၁ည်း—

把 "阿姆里薩" 的大慘殺咖
殘念無道的英國,是全亞細亞
類的敵人!

千九百十八年 四月十三日 インド ノ アムリッサノ
コウエンニ アツマッタ ツミノ ナイ ミンシ。ウニ
ムカッテ エイコクグンタイハ イキナリ キクッン
ジュウヲ ウチアビセ、ツヒニ 五百ニンモ コロシテ
シマヒ、二千ニンニ ヒドイ キズヲ アタヘタ。

In the little city of Amritsar in Punjab, India, on April 13, 1918, Britain was accredited with the world's bloodiest crime ever to be com-mitted by any civilized nation- the Amritsar Massacre.

Some five thousand innocent Indians on that day had gathered in the Jalianwalla Park to celebrate the Hindu New Year. British officials deemed this gathering as unlawful and without a word of warning ordered the guards to fire into the crowd which had gathered for the occasion. As machine guns sputtered, hundreds of Indians fell and when the sound of the guns had finally subsided, bullet-riddled bodies, by the hundreds, were strewn all over the blood stained ground. More than four hundred in-nocent Indians were murdered in cold-blood, while thousands of others seriously injured.

April 13 has left an indelible memory to all living Indians, never to be forgotten and never to be forgiven. The day, April 13, is observed as the day of national
people for the unfortu

The cold-blooded Am
fail to arouse fiery indig
Asiatics for it was typi
ty and savagery dealt
British. Such British a
ever, did not end on
parts of Asia which has

Within the image:

…T!

…ndian
…d not
…other
…cruel-
…ofthe
…how-
…n all
…etch-

ing claws of ruthless British rule, repeated acts
of similar nature have been committed against
the Asiatics in untold numbers.

阿姆里薩事件是發生在一九一八年
四月十三日，在印度盤扎布州首府阿姆
里薩的印度人，約有五千名，為慶祝印度
教的新年,當齊集在加里安瓦拉公園時,
忽然被英國官憲借不法集合的罪名,倉

未加以警告,即用機關槍四面掃射,演成
了死傷千數百名的慘劇從那一天起,四
月十八日便成了印度民族的哀悼日,在
實際上也是使我們東亞民族燃起熱血
沸騰的義憤的一天,英國在亞州各地作
這類似的行為,極其多的,恨,那是我們永
遠不能忘掉的。

98

98 A Japanese propaganda poster aimed
at turning Indian soldiers against the
British during the Second World War:

*In the little city of Amritsar in Punjab,
India, on April 13, 1918 [sic], Britain was
accredited with the world's bloodiest crime
ever to be committed by any civilized
nation - the Amritsar Massacre.*

*Some five thousand innocent Indians on
that day had gathered in the Jalianwalla
Park to celebrate the Hindu New Year.
British officials deemed this gathering as
unlawful and without a word of warning
ordered the guards to fire into the crowd
which had gathered for the occasion. As
machine guns sputtered, hundreds of
Indians fell and when the sound of the
guns had finally subsided, bullet-riddled
bodies, by the hundreds, were strewn
all over the blood stained ground. More
than four hundred innocent Indians were
murdered in cold-blood, while thousands
of others seriously injured.April 13 has left
an indelible memory to all living Indians,
never to be forgotten and never to be
forgiven. The day, April 13, is observed as
the day of national mourning by all Indian
people for the unfortunate victims.*

*The cold-blooded Amritsar Massacre did
not fail to arouse fiery indignations among
all other Asiatics for it was typical of the
kind of cruelty and savagery dealt out
by the hands of the British. Such British
acts of barbarism, however, did not end
on April 13, 1918 [sic]. In all parts of
Asia which has come under the stretching
claws of ruthless British rule, repeated acts
of similar nature have been committed
against the Asiatics in untold numbers.*

‘ The only amends that the British bureaucracy here or the British people in England have made for these acts is to ask us "to forgive and forget" the past, and sometime, when we feel inclined to close up this chapter of shame of our history, the cry that comes out of this blood-stained wall rings louder and clearer in our ears. It is always the cry of "Remember and avenge". ’

WILLIAM 'PUSSYFOOT' JOHNSON, AN AMERICAN VISITOR TO INDIA IN 1921, WAS TOLD BY HIS LOCAL GUIDE WHAT JALLIANWALA BAGH MEANT TO INDIANS.

EPILOGUE:
THE MEMORIAL

99 A rare photograph of Jallianwala Bagh in the 1930s, when it had been turned into a memorial park. Taken from a house in the south-eastern corner, the main entrance in the northern wall is centre-right of the image, where the path begins. The well is just visible under the small structure to the very right, while the shrine is hidden behind the trees on the far left.

99

100 In this aerial view of Amritsar taken in the
1930s, the Jallianwala Bagh memorial park
is visible in the bottom left corner.

'Can we afford to forget those five hundred or more men who were killed although they had done nothing wrong either morally or legally? If they had died knowingly and willingly, if realising their innocence they had stood their ground and faced the shots from the fifty rifles, they would have gone down to history as saints, heroes and patriots. But even as it was, the tragedy became one of first class national importance....

We were unable to protect our helpless countrymen when they were ruthlessly massacred. We may decline, if we will, to avenge the wrong. The nation will not lose if we did. But shall we – can we afford to – decline to perpetuate the memory and to show to the surviving members of the families of the dead that we are sharers in their sufferings, by erecting a national tombstone and by telling the world thereby that in the death of these men each one of us has lost dear relations?'

IN 1920, GANDHI PLAYED A KEY ROLE IN ESTABLISHING A MEMORIAL AT JALLIANWALA BAGH.

101 The official entrance to the Jallianwala Bagh Memorial. It became independent India's first national memorial in 1951.

Overleaf:

102 The Jallianwala Bagh Memorial today. The sculpture was designed by the American designer and architect, Benjamin Polk in 1956 and unveiled on 13 April 1961.

‘ In the ordinary English primer the only thing the ordinary person learns about British rule in India is about the Blackhole of Calcutta and the massacre of Cawnpore, where there was a well choked with corpses. Centuries hence you will find Indian children brought up to this spot. Just as they visit now the Cawnpore Well, and you can imagine the feelings of these Indians for generations over this terrible business.… Think what all this means! You will have a shrine erected there and every year there will be processions of Indians visiting the tombs of the martyrs and Englishmen will go there and stand bareheaded before it. ’

COMMENTS MADE BY THE RADICAL LABOUR POLITICIAN, J. C. WEDGWOOD, IN THE HOUSE OF COMMONS ON 22 DECEMBER 1919.

SOURCES

ILLUSTRATIONS

References given below relate to image nos:

1. Royal Geographical Society (with IBG)
2. John Hay Library, Brown University
3. Toor Collection
4. Toor Collection
5. Maynard Owen Williams, NG Image Collection
6. Toor Collection
7. Courtesy of Sikh Heritage Museum of Canada (Nanaki and Sahib Nagra Collected Works)
8. Copyright © The British Library Board. All Rights Reserved (9083.bb.12 facing p.76)
9. UKPHA Archive
10. Gordon Family Collection
11. Gordon Family Collection
12. Dinodia Photos / Alamy Stock Photo
13. Private Collection
14. Private Collection
15. Private Collection
16. Private Collection
17. Private Collection
18. Copyright © The British Library Board. All Rights Reserved (Photo 39(49))
19. Copyright © The British Library Board. All Rights Reserved (Photo 39(47))
20. Copyright © The British Library Board. All Rights Reserved (Photo 39(54))
21. Toor Collection
22. Copyright © The British Library Board. All Rights Reserved (Photo 39(80))
23. © Illustrated London News Ltd/Mary Evans
24. Copyright © The British Library Board. All Rights Reserved (Photo 39(66))
25. Copyright © The British Library Board. All Rights Reserved (Photo 39(78))
26. Copyright © The British Library Board. All Rights Reserved (Photo 39(58))
27. Copyright © The British Library Board. All Rights Reserved (Photo 39(61))
28. © Illustrated London News Ltd/Mary Evans
29. Collection of Kim A. Wagner
30. TopFoto
31. Private Collection
32. Copyright © The British Library Board. All Rights Reserved (Photo 39(63))
33. Copyright © The British Library Board. All Rights Reserved (Photo 39(87))
34. Percy Chisnall photo album, courtesy of Amanda Stacey
35. Percy Chisnall photo album, courtesy of Amanda Stacey
36. Percy Chisnall photo album, courtesy of Amanda Stacey
37. Percy Chisnall photo album, courtesy of Amanda Stacey
38. Percy Chisnall photo album, courtesy of Amanda Stacey
39. Royal Geogaphical Society (with IBG)
40. Private Collection
41. Courtesy of the Nehru Memorial Museum and Library
42. Courtesy of the Nehru Memorial Museum and Library
43. Courtesy of the Nehru Memorial Museum and Library
44. Courtesy of the Nehru Memorial Museum and Library
45. Private Collection
46. Percy Chisnall photo album, courtesy of Amanda Stacey
47. Copyright © The British Library Board. All Rights Reserved (Photo 39(81))
48. Copyright © The British Library Board. All Rights Reserved (Photo 39(82))
49. Copyright © The British Library Board. All Rights Reserved (Photo 39(83))
50. Courtesy of the Nehru Memorial Museum and Library
51. Courtesy of the Nehru Memorial Museum and Library
52. Copyright © The British Library Board. All Rights Reserved (Photo 39(84))
53. Private Collection
54. Private Collection
55. Courtesy of the Nehru Memorial Museum and Library
56. Copyright © The British Library Board. All Rights Reserved (Mss Eur C340/10(29–49))
57. Private Collection

58. Private Collection

59. TopFoto

60. TopFoto

61. TopFoto

62. TopFoto

63. Copyright © The British Library Board. All Rights Reserved (Mss Eur C340/10(29–49))

64. Copyright © The British Library Board. All Rights Reserved (Mss Eur C340/10(29–49))

65. Copyright © The British Library Board. All Rights Reserved (Mss Eur C340/10(29–49))

66. TopFoto

67. Copyright © The British Library Board. All Rights Reserved (Mss Eur C340/10(29–49))

68. Private Collection

69. Dinodia Photos / Alamy Stock Photo

70. Courtesy of the Nehru Memorial Museum and Library

71. British Empire and Commonwealth Collections, Bristol Archives, UK / Winthrop Collection / Bridgeman Images

72. Alinari Archives, Florence / Bridgeman Images

73. Dinodia Photos / Alamy Stock Photo

74. Private Collection

75. Courtesy of the Nehru Memorial Museum and Library

76. Courtesy of the Nehru Memorial Museum and Library

77. Dinodia Photos / Alamy Stock Photo

78. Private Collection

79. Private Collection

80. Private Collection

81. Private Collection

82. Copyright © The British Library Board. All Rights Reserved (IOR/L/PJ/6/1650, File 787)

83. Associated Newspapers/REX/Shutterstock

84. © Illustrated London News Ltd/Mary Evans

85. © Illustrated London News Ltd/Mary Evans

86. © Illustrated London News Ltd/Mary Evans

87. © Illustrated London News Ltd/Mary Evans

88. National Army Museum, London

89. National Army Museum, London

90. National Army Museum, London

91. ©John Frost Newspapers/Mary Evans Picture Library

92. Private Collection

93. Copyright © The British Library Board. All Rights Reserved (14158.de.28(5))

94. © Kim Wagner

95. Private Collection

96. National Army Museum, London

97. National Army Museum, London

98. Trustees of the Liddell Hart Centre for Military Archives

99. Courtesy of Hardeep Singh, Sandeep Singh Collection

100. Copyright © The British Library Board. All Rights Reserved (Photo 894/4(50))

101. TopFoto

102. © Kim Wagner

QUOTES

References given below relate to page nos:

EPIGRAPH

iv. Hugh Tinker, *The Ordeal of Love: C.F. Andrews and India* (Delhi: Oxford University Press, 1979), p 159; and B. R. Nanda, *The Nehrus: Motilal and Jawaharlal* (London: George Allen, 1962), p 168.

PRELUDE

18. *War Speeches of His Honour Sir Michael O'Dwyer, G.C.I.E., K.C.S.I., Lieutenant-Governor of the Punjab* (Lahore: Superintendent Government Printing, Punjab, 1918), p 118.

ROWLATT UNREST

34. Lady Lawrence [Rosamund Napier], *Indian Embers* (Oxford: George Ronald, 1949), pp 381–82.

37. *Disorders Inquiry Committee 1919–20, Evidence: vol. II* (Calcutta: His Majesty's Stationery Office, 1920), p 108.

39. *Amritsar Conspiracy Case*, National Archives of India, Acc No 1829 (Microfilm), p 106.

10–12 APRIL

42. V. N. Datta (ed), *New Light on the Punjab Disturbances in 1919: Volumes VI and VII of Disorders Inquiry Committee Evidence*, 2 vols (Simla: Indian Institute for Advanced Studies, 1975), vol 1, p 39.

45. (top) *Congress Punjab Inquiry 1919–1920, vol. II: Evidence* (Lahore: K. Santanam, 1920), p 720.

45. (bottom) Saadat Hasan Manto, 'A Tale of the Year 1919', in *My Name is Radha: The Essential Manto* (Gurgaon: Penguin India, 2015), p 203.

46. *Disorders Inquiry Committee 1919–20, Evidence: vol. III* (Calcutta: His Majesty's Stationery Office, 1920), p 42.

47. *Congress Punjab Inquiry 1919–1920, vol. II: Evidence*, pp 41–2.

48. Punjab State Archives (Chandigarh), 5315: Home Judicial, C, May 1920, nos 268-322, pp 2–3.

51. *Congress Punjab Inquiry 1919–1920, vol. II: Evidence*, p 137.

53. *Punjab Disturbances: Compiled from the Civil and Military Gazette* (Lahore: Civil and Military Gazette Press, 1919), p 11.

56. Punjab State Archives (Chandigarh), 5268: Home Judicial, B, June 1919, nos 249–70, p 1.

60. 'Amritsar – April 1919', Papers of Brigadier F. M. McCallum, Centre for South Asian Studies, Cambridge, p 1.

63. *Congress Punjab Inquiry 1919–1920, vol. II: Evidence*, pp 1–2.

67. Muhammad Ashraf Khan quoted in *Amritsar Conspiracy Case*, National Archives of India, Acc No 1829 (Microfilm), p 109.

13 APRIL

68. Muhammad Ashraf Khan quoted in *Amritsar Conspiracy Case*, National Archives of India, Acc No 1829 (Microfilm), p 109.

70. Appendix I, *Disorders Inquiry Committee 1919–20, Evidence: vol. III*, p 212.

71. Appendix II, ibid.

74. K. D. Malaviya, *Open Rebellion in Punjab* (Allahabad, 1920), pp 4–5.

75. *Congress Punjab Inquiry 1919–1920, vol. II: Evidence*, p 80.

78. (top) Ibid, p 93.

78. (bottom) Ibid, p 68.

79. 'The Amritsar Resolution, Law Report, 26 May 1924: High Court of Justice', *The Times*, 27 May 1924.

82. Command 771 (Disturbances in the Punjab): Statement by Brig.-General R. E. Dyer, C.B. (London, 1920), p 7.

85. *Disorders Inquiry Committee 1919–20, Evidence: vol. III*, pp 202–03.

86. Command 771 (Disturbances in the Punjab): Statement by Brig.-General R.E. Dyer, C.B. (London, 1920), Appendix A, p 25.

89. Ibid, p 19.

92. Rupert Furneaux, 'The Massacre at Amritsar', *Times Literary Supplement*, 9 April 1964.

93. *Congress Punjab Inquiry 1919–1920, vol. II: Evidence*, p 68.

94–5. Ibid, p 112.

96. *Disorders Inquiry Committee 1919–20, Evidence: vol. III*, p 203.

97. *Congress Punjab Inquiry 1919–1920, vol. II: Evidence*, pp 9–10.

101. Ibid, p 91.

102. Ibid, p 11.

104–05. Command 771 (Disturbances in the Punjab): Statement by Brig.-General R.E. Dyer, C.B. (London, 1920), Appendix C, pp 27–8.

106–07. *Congress Punjab Inquiry 1919–1920, vol. II: Evidence*, pp 117–18.

MARTIAL LAW

108. *Disorders Inquiry Committee 1919–20, Evidence: vol. III*, p 120.

110. *Congress Punjab Inquiry 1919–1920, vol. II: Evidence*, p. 14.

111. Ibid, p 182.

114. *Disorders Inquiry Committee 1919–20, Evidence: vol. III*, p 207.

116. *Congress Punjab Inquiry 1919–1920, vol. II: Evidence*, p 24.

118. (top) *Disorders Inquiry Committee 1919–20, Evidence: vol. III*, p 205.

118. (bottom) *Congress Punjab Inquiry 1919–1920, vol. II: Evidence*, p 164.

122. (top) Ibid, p 171.

122. (bottom) *Disorders Inquiry Committee 1919–20, Evidence: vol. III*, p 124.

124. *Congress Punjab Inquiry 1919–1920, vol. II: Evidence*, p 114.

AFTERMATH

128. *Hansard*, HC, Deb 8 July 1920, vol 131, col 1725.

130. C. Dewey, *Anglo-Indian Attitudes: The Mind of the Indian Civil Service* (London: Hambledon Press, 1993), p 161.

131. R. Trevelyan, *The Golden Oriole* (London: Secker & Warburg, 1987), pp 482, 485.

133. I. Colvin, *The Life of General Dyer* (Edinburgh: William Blackwood & Sons, 1929), p 202.

135. *The Statesman*, 3 June 1919.

137. (top) Report by Sant Singh, National Archives of India, Home Political, Deposit, September 1919, no 12.

137. (bottom) Pearay Mohan, *An Imaginary Rebellion: and how it was Suppressed: An Account of the Punjab Disorders and the Working of the Martial Law* (Lahore: Khosla Bros, 1920), p 370.

144. *The Collected Works of Mahatma Gandhi*, 98 vols (Ahmedabad: The Publication Division, 1965), vol 16, p 313.

147. K. D. Malaviya, *Open Rebellion in Punjab*, pp 62–3.

150. *Report of the Committee appointed by the Government of India to investigate the disturbances in the Punjab, etc. (Disorders Inquiry Committee 1919–20)* (Calcutta: His Majesty's Stationery Office, 1920), p 150. 'Minority Report', p 115.

151. Letter dated 14 July 1920, The National Archives of the UK (Kew), WO 32/21403.

152. 'General Dyer', *Daily Mail*, 5 May 1920.

156. *Hansard*, HC, Deb 8 July 1920, vol 131, col 1713.

157. Ibid.

160. 'For Gen. Dyer', *Morning Post*, 8 July 1919.

161. *The Collected Works of Mahatma Gandhi*, vol 18, pp 45–6.

163. 'The Man Who Saved India', *Morning Post*, 28 July 1927.

166. Letters to the Editor, *Westminster Gazette*, 27 July 1927.

PICTURING THE MASSACRE

168. Quoted from a propaganda poster titled 'Remember the Amritsar Incident!' (Trustees of the Liddell Hart Centre for Military Archives).

172. Manohar Lal Shukla, *Julmi Dyer ya Jaliyanvala Bagh* (Kanpur, 1922), p 25.

EPILOGUE: THE MEMORIAL

182. Tarini Prasad Sinha, *"Pussyfoot" Johnson and His Campaign in Hindustan* (Madras: Ganesh & Co, 1922), p 243.

189. 'Jallianwala Bagh', *Young India*, 18 February 1920, p 3.

192. *Hansard*, HC, Deb 22 December 1919, vol 123, cols 1231–32.

BACK COVER

Churchill: *Hansard*, HC, Deb 8 July 1920, vol 131, col 1725.

Tagore: Tagore to Andrews, 22 July 1920, in *Rabindranath Tagore, Letters to a Friend* (London: George Allen & Unwin, 1926), p 87.

Gandhi: *The Collected Works of Mahatma Gandhi*, vol 18, pp 45–6.

FURTHER READINGS

For the most forensically gripping account of the Amritsar Massacre yet written, we recommend Kim A. Wagner's *Amritsar 1919: An Empire of Fear and the Making of a Massacre* (London: Yale University Press, 2019; published in South Asia as *Jallianwala Bagh: An Empire of Fear and the Making of the Amritsar Massacre*, New Delhi: Penguin, 2019).

The following works cover a range of topics relevant to the events of 1919:

A. Anand, *The Patient Assassin: A True Tale of Massacre, Revenge and the Raj* (London: Simon & Schuster, 2019).

N. Collett, *The Butcher of Amritsar: Brigadier-General Reginald Dyer* (London: Continuum, 2006).

V. N. Datta and S. Settar (eds), *Jallianwala Bagh Massacre* (Delhi: Pragati Publications: Indian Council of Historical Research, 2000).

E. M. Forster, *A Passage to India* (London: Edward Arnold, 1924; new edn, London: Penguin, 2005).

S. H. Manto, *My Name is Radha: The Essential Manto* (Gurgaon: Penguin India, 2015).

G. Orwell, *Burmese Days* (London: Victor Gollancz, 1935; new edn, London: Penguin, 2014).

C. Pinney, *The Coming of Photography in India* (New Delhi: Oxford University Press, 2008).

D. Sayer, 'British Reactions to the Amritsar Massacre, 1919–1920', *Past & Present*, 131, 1 (May 1991), pp 130–64.

T. C. Sherman, *State Violence and Punishment in India* (New York: Routledge, 2009).

K. L. Tuteja, 'Jallianwala Bagh: A Critical Juncture in the Indian National Movement', *Social Scientist*, xxv, 1/2 (January–February 1997), pp 25–61.

ACKNOWLEDGEMENTS

SPECIAL THANKS

We owe a monumental debt of gratitude to the world's foremost expert on the Amritsar Massacre – Kim A. Wagner. His incredible research, editorial insights, co-curation and generosity of spirit have been fundamental to the creative endeavour that gave rise to *Eyewitness at Amritsar*. We hope that this book will serve as a complementary volume to his brilliantly conceived and recently released *Amritsar 1919: An Empire of Fear and the Making of a Massacre*.

Our thanks also go out to friends and colleagues who lent us their invaluable support. Paul Smith (paulsmithdesign.com) has brought the events of 1919 into sharp, chilling focus through his meticulous design work. On the research front, Jasdeep Singh gave critical assistance by tracing images from the collections of the National Army Museum, London. Similarly, thanks to Iqbal Husain for his help in locating a letter from The National Archives at Kew. Dr Bikram Brar cast his expert editorial eye over the text while Baljinder Singh Grewal and Sukhdeep Singh Jodha skilfully translated texts from Hindi, Punjabi and Urdu. We are extremely grateful to all of the institutions and individuals who gave permission to allow us to reproduce their images in the book. In particular, we are indebted to members of the Gordon Family – namely Hilary Bach, Peter Hopcraft and his daughter Caroline – who were quick to grant permission to reproduce images from the family's invaluable photograph album relating to the 15th Sikhs during the First World War. Thanks too to our dear friend, Eleanor Nesbitt, who shared valuable source material from her book *Sikh: Two Centuries of Western Women's Art & Writing* (Kashi House, forthcoming 2019).

Finally, we would like to thank our wives, Harpreet and Dilgir, for their unstinting support and our kids – Nirlep, Khem, Suhavi, Jup, Saroop and Sekunder – for making us realise that they need to see and hear our stories.

A NOTE ABOUT THE EDITORS

AMANDEEP SINGH MADRA and PARMJIT SINGH are independent historians and curators who co-founded the UK Punjab Heritage Association (ukpha.org), a charity dedicated to promoting Punjab's rich cultural heritage. Parmjit Singh is also a co-founder and managing editor of Kashi House CIC.

They have co-authored several acclaimed books on Sikh history and are leading global players in showcasing the culture, history, art and heritage of the Sikhs and Punjab. They have lectured extensively on the subject as well as having contributed to several television documentaries, radio programmes, exhibitions and publications. They have curated three major exhibitions at the Brunei Gallery, SOAS, London, exploring the Golden Temple of Amritsar (2011), Sikhs in World War One (2014) and the Sikh Empire (2018).

They continue to work as special consultants for various organisations that have included the BBC, The Discovery Channel, Victoria & Albert Museum, British Museum, British Library and Wallace Collection.

ABOUT THE PUBLISHER

KASHI HOUSE CIC is the only mainstream publisher in the world dedicated to producing high quality books on the rich cultural heritage of the Sikhs and Punjab. Established as a not-for-profit social enterprise in 2006, all profits are reinvested in new projects.

IN PURSUIT OF EMPIRE: TREASURES FROM THE TOOR COLLECTION OF SIKH ART
By Davinder Toor
The remarkable story of the Sikh Empire told through a spectacular selection of over 100 rare and beautiful objects from the world's finest collection of Sikh art

1984: INDIA'S GUILTY SECRET
By Pav Singh
'Nowhere else in the world did the year 1984 fulfil its apocalyptic portents as it did in India' – Amitav Ghosh

THE TARTAN TURBAN: IN SEARCH OF ALEXANDER GARDNER
By John Keay
'Minutely researched, wittily written and beautifully produced, it is one of John Keay's most memorable achievements' – William Dalrymple

For further details of our books, authors, art prints & events visit:
kashihouse.com
facebook.com/kashihouse
twitter.com/kashihouse
instagram.com/kashihousecic

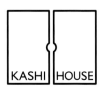